For You, Lili Marlene

For You, Lili Marlene

A MEMOIR OF WORLD WAR II

Robert Peters

The University of Wisconsin Press

A NORTH COAST BOOK

The University of Wisconsin Press
114 North Murray Street
Madison, Wisconsin 53715

3 Henrietta Street
London WC2E 8LU, England

2 4 6 8 10 9 7 5 3 1

Printed in the United States of America

Library of Congress Cataloging-in-Publication Data
Peters, Robert, 1924–
For you, Lili Marlene: a memoir of World War II / Robert Peters.
    122 p.   cm.
Continues: Peters, Robert. Crunching gravel.
    ISBN 0-299-14810-6 (alk. paper)
1. Peters, Robert, 1924–   . 2. World War, 1939–1945—Personal
4. Soldiers—United States—Biography.   I. Peters, Robert, 1924–
            D811.P4676   1995
                811′.54—dc20
            [B]   95-13155

*To the men of Company D, 422nd Regiment,
106th Infantry Division, with whom I trained, and most
of whom were killed or taken prisoner during the
Battle of the Bulge, and for my children
Rob, Meredith, Richard, Cathy, and Jefferson*

Let the naturalists explain these things, and the reason and manner of them. All I can say to them is to describe the fact, which was even surprising to me when I found it . . .
—Daniel DeFoe, *Robinson Crusoe*

Make the little man march
make the little man hate
make the little man kill.
—Charles Plymell, "Star Tattoo
Dying on the Day-Glo"

One thinks to escape, but doesn't, or not wholly: the fingerprints were taken early on. The past recurs in which unfulfilled, half-forgotten lusts explode.
—Patrick White, *Flaws in the Glass*

Contents

Note

No POPULAR song of World War II better encapsulated the war than "Lili Marlene," which both sides in the conflict found equally stirring. For the Allies, the song belonged to Marlene Dietrich, who was indefatigable in performing it before huge audiences of GIs in Paris and elsewhere. I attended one of her most memorable concerts. That Paris evening in 1944 remains as vivid to me as though it has just happened.

Preface

DECEMBER 8, 1941, the day following Pearl Harbor, was frigid. Despite the sun, the thermometer outside our kitchen window recorded thirty degrees below zero. My breath formed frost crystals on my face and scarf as I scurried for the warmth of Tony Dolansky's school bus. Forty-five minutes later we reached the high school, still unaware of the news.

At 9:30, Principal E. V. Kracht assembled us in the gymn to hear the president address Congress and the nation. One hundred and thirty of us jammed the balcony overlooking the basketball court. There was horseplay until Mr. Kracht quieted us and plugged in a radio.

As Roosevelt's voice, edged with rage, recounted the events of the "day of infamy," declaring war on Japan, there were bowed heads. "Your lives will never be the same," Mr. Kracht declared. "Now, return to classes."

That June I slicked my hair with brilliantine, traversed the high school gym, and received my diploma. For nearly two years I worked as a file clerk for the Employers' Mutual Insurance Company, in Wausau. In March 1943, I quit my job and spent a week with my family before going to war.

I shall strive for candor, to tell what I remember of those years and to delineate the complex sexual and social forces that shaped my psyche when I left the sheltered Wisconsin farm for the war. My book is as much the story of my struggle for self-knowledge as it is an account of that part of World War II I saw and survived. Those years, my own "animal soup of time," profoundly determined what I am today. My sense of the connection between sexuality and military life may, I hope, contribute to an as yet imperfectly understood phenomena. I'll leave it to the theorists to speculate on how the freneticisms engendered in sensitive young male minds by the dislocations, threats of maimings and death, and fevered patriotism of war intensify testosterone levels to a degree seldom seen in civilian lives. To see guns and bayonets as phalluses, and beautiful youths "dying" in war as victims of sexual atrocities are, of course, clichés.

Huntington Beach
August 1, 1994

For You, Lili Marlene

1

Wisconsin

T HE LIVER-colored train took over two hours to make the sixty-mile run from Wausau, a single daily northward route eschewing straight lines. Waits at obscure depots seemed interminable. At last I stepped out into fresh snow at Eagle River. Until mid-May a blizzard could appear at anytime. To my left, facing Wall Street, were the remains of an ice palace designed by Hanke's Coal Company using ice-blocks from the local river. Some of the greenish edifice was melting and the fairy-tale turrets had already crumbled. As the train disappeared through a stand of spruce, the final car glinted with a cold light. The village, for it was hardly more than that, struck me as diminished from what it had been, when a three-mile walk into town was an event and the cluster of false-front, turn-of-the-century buildings of corrugated tin seemed cosmopolitan, even huge.

"Did you know the Jolly boy?"

"Which one?" I asked.

"There's four in the service," the station man said. "The one that's in the Navy died. We heard yesterday. Think it was Bill. Now that family's doin' its part . . . "

"I know them," I said, buttoning my coat.

"Are you in the war?"

"I've been drafted," I said.

At the Sundstein Road I crossed a small trestle over black, swirling Mud Creek. We'd always assumed large pike and pickerel swam there, but all we ever hooked were stunted rock bass. Steam rose from the mix of cold water and warm air. Patch ice clung to reeds and willow branches along the banks.

I passed the Ludwig farm. The grey house with its steep dormers was sinking into the swamp. Outbuildings had collapsed. A farmer in a

3

pickup passed—Henry Ollerby with his wife and four plump daughters. Sand Corner. A trash dump of rusted cans and old bedsprings. Juneberry shrubs. Spruce, pine, and hemlock. No deciduous trees were yet in leaf, although maples and pussy willows were budding. A buck snorted, his white-flag tail raised. Soughs of wind. In the road, silvery clods of snow tinged with gravel. Glare-ice in the swamps. Partridge tracks crisscrossed a rabbit trail. Where the partridge, startled, took flight wing tips etched the snow.

I wanted to surprise my folks with news of a marriage—mine, to prove that I was a man. Not for lack of trying was I trudging home alone, for I had proposed to four women. All had rejected me. Lilly Swift, who resembled Linda Darnell, sold tickets at a movie house in Wausau, one specializing in third-rate cowboy films. I saw Orson Welles' *Citizen Kane* there. Even in this worst of cinemas the film's run was stopped after two nights—audiences hooted and screamed, demanding their money back. Lilly refused my requests for dates, until, finally, she agreed to a visit. She was sitting in a wicker chair on her front porch, wearing a white blouse and a peasant skirt.

"I've had polio," she said. "I wear a brace."

I took her hand.

"So, you see," she said.

Blonde Marge Kendall had a weekly radio program devoted to household hints interspersed with popular songs. While she said she liked me, she laughed at the idea of sharing my bed. She never wasted sentiments. "And what if you come back without legs," she said, "or without some other vital parts? What's a girl in wartime to do?" Betty Aaron was a math wizard and valedictorian. She was also skeptical of religions, which bothered me since I was a devout Lutheran. I put myself through silly but intense prayers for her conversion. Raven-haired Helen Teiger suggested we do more than kiss. I was distressed. During one of our late-night trysts on a tacky couch on her front porch, she asked me if I preferred boys. She liked biting me.

From the house itself a thin trail of smoke rose from a metal pipe secured to the roof with haywire. Globs of cold tar dripped from the chinking between side-wall logs perpendicular to the ground. The squat building looked scoured with grime. Every log had been harvested, hewn, and placed by my father. His powerful hands had set every flange and nail. I passed the birch-pole garage.

4

Mom was in the kitchen baking pancakes. She was slender, black-haired, and wore a dress with faded roses and an oversized green sweater. Jane, Nell, and Everett, my siblings, were at the round oak table.

"It's Bob!" Jane shouted, jumping up.

Mom dropped her turner. "I knew you'd come," she said. "Get Dad, Nell. He's at the barn."

"I'll go," I said.

Dad was forking cow dung through a trap door giving on to a huge mound of straw and manure, for fertilizing crops. He would also excavate the family outhouse which stood nearby, reserving those nitrogen-rich deposits for prized vegetables and strawberries.

"I'll be damned," said Dad, smiling.

"I'm here for breakfast," I said.

"Let's water the cow first. She's thirsty."

I unchained Lady and her bull calf. Anxious to be free, they plunged through melting snow towards the well and a steaming half-barrel of water.

The breakfast was one my family ate nearly every morning: pancakes from sour batter kept fermenting on the back of the wood stove, side pork, fried potatoes, and eggs soaked in bacon grease. We topped the pancakes with thick cream and either sugar, blueberry jam, or Karo syrup. My parents drank coffee so strong it was almost sludge.

"How long can you stay?" Mom asked, clearing the table.

"Ten days." I would be sent East for basic training, where exactly I didn't know.

"We'll make the most of your visit," she said.

The cotton mattress on my old bed sagged on a grid of baling wire and was covered with crazy quilts fashioned by my mother from cloth scraps. My favorite had zigzag lightning shapes sewn to a plain backing of ecru flannel. The bed fit neatly into a corner of a hip-roofed attic room, near a small window giving onto the front yard. The walls remained unfinished—bare planking with protruding nail-ends securing the flimsy tar paper to the outside roof. In winter, frost formed around these nails, and as the house warmed from the heater downstairs the frost melted, dripping onto my face as I lay in bed. An apple crate, on end, with a faded cloth tacked to it, held a single-wick kerosene lamp and a box of matches. In the crate was my old Bible.

After returning to town for my suitcase, I helped Dad clear an acre of woodlot for a new field. While one brush pile burned, we moved to others cut and piled before snow fell, trimmings from the trees Dad had harvested for winter fuel.

On Sunday, after the Lutheran service, I spoke with Rev. Beckler, a severe figure with powerful fists and a guttural voice who was enamored of Original Sin. At the very moment of rupturing your mother's amniotic sac, he maintained, you had automatically broken all Ten Commandments. I had been superintendent of his Sunday school, proselytizing his ideas, overwhelming the youthful minds in my charge. I believed the Bible explicitly, including the commandment "Thou shalt not kill." My goal was then to become a minister, something Beckler said would take more money than I had. The congregation lacked the funds to support me at a seminary.

"You'll serve your country well, Robert. I know that. Do remember, though, that if you are to avoid Eternal Damnation unto yourself, you must never take Holy Communion from other than a Missouri Synod minister. I shall expect you to write me for a special dispensation before receiving the consecrated wafer and wine from any other hands."

I visited my old math teacher and forensic coach Esther Austin, who lived near the high school. We sat in her brown living room filled with decaying furniture. Esther, who never married, was short and stout, and had mannishly cropped gray hair. She peered up at me from her rocker, smiling. She had been a second mother and, though I was unaware of it, had kept a meticulous journal on my growth and behavior throughout my high school years. She realized early that I was ill-synchronized with others my age, felt inferior because of my impoverished farm origins, and was a child in most matters. It was true that I had matriculated in first grade when I was barely four years old.

Esther contrived "opportunities" for me to speak in class, coached me for oratory competitions, and saw me in her office where I brought gifts from home—a quart jar of canned chicken or venison, homemade jam, crude valentines. She kept a score of pluses and minuses regarding my maturation; the minuses meant steps backwards, the pluses steps forward. She was patient for signs of my lessening dependence on her. Since my awkwardness with girls bothered her she arranged for me to work on projects with girls she thought I might like. I would never have hinted to her of my attraction to boys.

Eventually she submitted her journal to the University of Wisconsin and received a master's degree in psychology. Before I left that afternoon she gave me a small pocket Bible. "Carry it over your heart," she said. The *Readers Digest* featured stories of soldiers, both from an Illinois town, she reported, who carried similar Bibles in their shirt pockets; the Bibles deflected enemy bullets. I pasted a colored photo of Durer's famous praying hands over the title page, and carried the book through basic training, maneuvers, and Europe.

I also visited Mrs. Jolly who owned the last farm on Sundstein Road. In her front window was a framed gold star commemorating Bill, the son killed on a destroyer in the Atlantic. Her two youngest boys were still at home. Three others were in the service, safe so far as she knew. The house still had the comfortable disarray I had loved. Mrs. Jolly wore a shapeless, badly-dyed purple dress made of flour sacking. A few chickens chortled as they moved about the kitchen looking for food. Some flew onto the dining table.

"I'm so sorry about Bill," I said. He and his younger brother George were my close friends. Less loquacious than George, who was my age, huskier, with a quiet sense of humor, Bill always seemed more mature. Whenever I needed pointers on casting for trout, tapping maples, or solving algebra problems, I asked Bill. During our summer visits to Lake Seventeen for swimming, he never flaunted his nudity as George did. In the Jolly's barn one summer I discovered sex.

"Yes," Mrs. Jolly said, seating herself at the kitchen table. "Bill wanted to go. He tried to enlist, but the draft got him. Wish he'd gone to the marines. That's what he wanted. The navy killed him." She paused. "You two was friends, I know." She held out a clipping from the weekly paper. "That's how he looked in his uniform. So handsome. He came home briefly, and then they assigned him to a boat carrying troops to Europe."

"We were close," I said, fumbling for words.

"I'm worried now about George," she went on. "He's headed for Europe, and the infantry. Be careful," she said, taking my hand when I got up to leave. "We need you back here."

At home, I asked Mom for the old scrapbooks we had made by clipping and pasting graphic World War I horror pictures from the *Milwaukee Journal* into old wallpaper sample books. These were images I recalled: a youth clutching his belly, his mouth agape, his head thrust back in agony; trench scenes of doughboys with rotten toes and feet livid with bacteria; two horses mangled in a no-man's land of barbed wire; another horse blown into a tree denuded of its primary branches; rats devouring the extremities of dead men; rats clambering over a bombed church altar, defiling a crucifix; defeated men with bandaged heads and limbs, assisted by comrades, seeking medics; a soldier writing home to his wife, who was shot sitting exactly where he was photographed; close-ups of mustard gas burns; refugees with personal possessions tied to their backs wending through disastrously ruined towns; a child grabbing the breasts of a dead mother; a flaming building.

"I burned those books," Mom said. "Page by page." She paused. She was washing dishes. "Those pictures didn't keep us out of war. I wanted the war to stop before you turned eighteen." She was reflective. "My brothers saw rats in those trenches, had their lungs destroyed by mustard gas. Men cause wars. Mothers want their sons to be peacemakers, dads want them to kill."

"Think," I said, "how that makes this son feel. How can I please both you and Dad?"

White arbutus peeped through patches of old snow, and in the ditches along the roads masses of jellied frog eggs glimmered. When I reached a sandy hill used by partridges for dusting, I stripped and lay on my back with my eyes closed, absorbing the sun. I lay there for over an hour.

Two days before induction, I borrowed a neighbor's canoe, launched it on a creek, and paddled it for several miles, toward Columbus Lake, where I had often fished with the Jollys.

My boyhood fear of forests was irrational. No bear had ever attacked anyone I knew. And while timber wolves could be heard baying on nights when the northern lights stained the Wisconsin skies, we had never observed wolf packs on the prowl. Rumored wild men of the forest remained that—we had never seen one wearing swamp reeds, or grass and ferns, the face swollen with wood ticks gorged on his blood. My fears were totemic. Fecund wood odors, I now realize, especially in dank forests where sunlight was excluded, were sexual. Ground muck, black and tarry, seemed to want to suck me in.

As I paddled the borrowed canoe, blisters soon formed on my hands and broke, smarting. To soothe them I dragged my fingers through the cold, iodine-rich water. My brain seemed suspended in time—a rag bag of needles clicking, clots of wool formed into yellow stars on a field of green. Illusions sailed past, neo-cortextual fermentations deflecting the claws of harpies, gas shells exploding over already ravaged terrain.

As I drifted beneath twisted hemlock, red ants fell, biting my neck. Tamarack dangled green hair, mossy, in webs. Fern croziers cracked through the lush soil of the banks. Buckwheat plants bloomed in streams of sun.

I passed beneath trees demolished by past storms. The dipping of my paddle seemed like the dipping of a spoon, a communion. Trees crowded in, and I moved by grabbing branches: the effect was like passing through an enormous chest cavity, a bronchial tangle, a heart system. The air was sweet with alcohol and blood. A hemlock branch struck my face, a residue of gum, pitch, on my cheek.

At a marsh of red moss I beached the canoe, and stepped out. Above me, anger seemed suddenly to blot the clouds. Had I understood the significance of my departure? I might never return home. My boots were soaked past the laces. I was in past my knees.

On returning to the canoe, I spied a large crane on a rock surrounded by pink air. Feathers swung from his scraggly neck. He scraped his beak on a wing, blinked, and kept staring. I grabbed a stone and flung it. A red eye swam, a bone cracked. Feathers fanned in the wind. A clash of bird screams, ice-bones shivering in a thaw.

I had had only one fistfight in my life, in Ashland, when I was nine. The boy, Garland Sweet, lived with his widowed, alcoholic mother in a shack outside the town. The local boys would strip off his pants and order him to lie on his belly. After whisking him with switches, they climbed on him, simulating sex.

One afternoon, Chuck Jones, a sixteen year old, actually sodomized Garland, and then forced the boy to rip carrots from his mother's garden and cook soup for us over an outdoor fire in a coffee can. We ate the soup, and, for good measure, pulled more carrots to eat on the way home. Before we departed, Chuck decided I should beat Garland. I refused—until Chuck threatened to beat me. He forced Garland's arms behind his back.

"Hit him in the mouth, Peters."

"Yes," shouted someone else, "if you don't we'll smash you."

Garland waited dumbly as I struck him. Then I ran home.

All during my adolescence, I had nightmares of attacks by hostile males. I always froze, unable even to get my hands up to protect myself. These dreams persisted into my teens.

I dreaded injury. In my Bible readings, I delighted in the image of

Jesus as passive, of a Father/God so caring that a single feather falling from a bird's body, or a hair from a baby's head, disturbed him. Jesus suffered and died so that I should never have to inflict pain. These conclusions reflected a profound self-failure. I displaced the violence, blood, and vengeance of the Old Testament for a marshmallow-faced Jesus, of the sort suspended above the altar in the Christ Evangelical Lutheran Church.

I had always pitied the farm animals we slaughtered, and seldom participated in butcherings. Whenever we killed a sow, I hid until Dad shot the animal, sliced its throat, immersed the carcass in a boiling mixture of lye and ashes, and gutted it. On one occasion Dad insisted that I help him.

A single shot stunned the sow at her trough of hot mash. I held the pan to catch the blood. Dad slashed the throat. Once we had dressed the pig and hung it up secure from coyotes, I took the head which Dad had thrust aside for our dog to eat and wrapped it in butcher paper. The late afternoon sky, I remember, was dun, chilled by a stiff breeze. I grabbed an axe and, carrying the head, set off for Mud Minnow Lake.

I could have wrapped the head more securely, for tucked beneath my arm it seeped juices. I shifted the burden to my other arm to ease the aching. What I was doing was wrong—Dad had meant for the meat to supplement the meager table scraps our dog usually ate. Dad would probably beat me. I hurried on, crossed shivering ice. In the deep, pure water I saw no heads, nor heard groans; there was only water, deep, and in the wintry mud beds I imagined hibernating frogs. Not a bush quivered. After crossing snow formations and wind-whipped encrusted ridges, I reached the center. I imagined depths where bass hovered, perch whirled fins, and bluegills soaked up heat. The muck itself was rich, the silt of leaves drifting, compacting over eons, forming lignite.

I knelt, chopping until I reached yellow water. Pus spilled as I widened the gash. Tchick! Tchick! Ice-chips flew. Water blew from the hole. My knees were stuck to the ice.

Dropping the axe, I reached for the head and unwrapped it. Its ears stood up. The snout with the Tinkertoy holes held blood. It's eyes were shut. A single oat grain stuck to its lower lip. I brought the head above the ice, dropped it through the hole, watched it sink and glimmer, a match wink.

Now, seated in the canoe, I considered the soft pad of flesh beneath my finger. Fingerprints reveal what a mirror can't. Here my linear self begins, I think; and all that I am, including what I shall become, runs in a line circling from here. Set to shiver, as in a moment of fear, my dermis caught an electric snap (feel it) faintly, a gluefast suction foot, octopus sense of a sea's tide, lake blood rippling beneath a fat water spider. Blood drops in the water! I had torn my hand. Soothing stream. Muskellunge and pike forms, spangled, streaking past. Margin of dusk, the brain's fallow land, and the dark sibilants of coming night. A muskellunge (a small one) struck for my finger, swirled and sank. It nerved past, hidden by a clutch of waterweeds. A stone nearby, immersed, shone like pure mica.

To reach the open lake, I slashed through weeds, striking black-seeded grass forms, wild rice, lilies, and decomposing evergreens. A forked branch resembled human arms. There was a figure on its back with its knees bent in fetal position. I brought it high loaded with scum, then flung it as far from me as I could. The water cleared. Swish and slash of weed spear. Scrape and tear of lily pad. The prow of the canoe rose. The paddle dripped blue silt. The air, cold sharp diamond, pricked my throat. My shirt was drenched. The north sky slid with ice light. A fresh wind clattered, shaking the reeds. Fish forms encased in water winked. The canoe was turning, creating vitrescent waves the color of cinnamon. Reed beds began again as ash-colored trees rose and fir trees bled green, charting the way home. A merganser croaked, banked, dropped its shadow over the boat, then struck north and disappeared. A bird's claw drew up a black lamp towards Cassiopeia. Night fell.

That evening, as I was packing, Dad gave me a knife he had crudely fashioned of polished aluminum with a haft to match. He had shaped it from a single metal bar retrieved from the town dump on one of his scavenger hunts for scrap metals to be sold for the war effort.

"You'll need to defend yourself, son," he said, nodding, handing over the weapon sheathed in a buckskin cover which my mother had ornamented with small colored beads in the Indian fashion. He had worked for hours crafting the knife, yet another link in a sequence of fathers blessing sons going to war. Even in a remote backwoods, such a cause ran deep—the blood and guts of the father reconstituted in the son for the good of the culture. An accident of birth had spared Dad

Holding sister Jane, Wisconsin, 1943.

With my parents Dorothy and Sam, in Sawyer, Wisconsin.

from war, a zodiacal timing. He was too young for World War I, and now was too old for World War II.

Despite Dad's efforts to seal and polish the knife, I was ashamed of it. The pair of aluminum protuberances he had welded on the underside resembled a pair of elf buttocks. The blade itself came from one of his favorite deer hunting knives and was so sharp, he boasted, that it could shave pussy.

"I wish I could be goin' instead of you," he said, expressing what thousands of fathers—German, Japanese, British, American—were undoubtedly expressing at the time. He was only twelve in 1914, and now, in the spring of 1943, he was forty-one. He'd offered to enlist, he boasted, but they wouldn't sign on an "old pup." Then, too, there was his arthritic back. He would "go to war" by brushing up his welding skills and "enlisting" in the shipyards in Sturgeon Bay, in northeastern Wisconsin. "I'm proud of you, son," he said, taking the knife from my hand and turning it before his face. "Just tie it to your leg with the leather strings, and when a Kraut comes at you, reach down, yank out the knife, and let him have it between the ribs . . . right here," he said, thumping his belly. "Strike it in," Dad said. "Like the Kraut was a deer."

The knife felt dead. I had no sense of how I could ever flip it from its sheath and plunge it through a German.

That night I waited until the family went to bed before finally packing the suitcase I'd need. A pair of slacks, a shirt, and a jacket would suffice until I was issued army clothes. I packed a few toilet articles, a razor, and a change of underwear and socks.

The suitcase was open on the kitchen table near a paper bag of oatmeal-raisin cookies Mom made for the trip. I would catch the train at 1:30 P.M.

I had not yet made up my mind to take the silver knife, although I knew that if I didn't Dad would be disappointed. I started for the stairs, intending to hide it near my bed, in the apple box where I kept the Bible. It would be invisible there, unless, of course, my brother Everett rummaged around, which was unlikely, since he hated reading.

At the foot of the stairs, I paused with the knife in my hand, the blade towards my fingers. With my free hand I tested it. A tap would break the skin.

I returned to the table, put the knife down, and from a nearby counter took a round of fresh venison, cut high on the haunch, that my mother would cook for dinner. It was the size of a man's upper thigh, though the purplish hue of the flesh was certainly not human.

Placing the haunch on butcher paper, I positioned it near the edge of the counter and began tracing the knife point along a tallow ridge. Then I positioned the knife for a thrust: if you were stabbing a man would you clasp the knife palm up so as to impale your victim with a slashing rip from low in the belly up towards the throat? Or would you clench your fingers, bringing your hand up in a forward motion, staggering the enemy with a single, stark blow? The latter would work best if you were close enough to pierce the heart; the former would be most efficient in feinting and parrying. I clenched the knife and waited, then thrust it to the hilt deep into the purple meat.

2

Basic Training:
March 1943–May 1944

URTLY, almost contemptuously, the doctor orders: "Pull it back! Skin it, farmer!" The stocky, red-haired boy from Merrill is immobilized as the MD grabs his penis and yanks back the foreskin. "See?" he exclaims. "Know what that's called, boy?" No response. "That's smega! There's enough head cheese to feed a platoon! Now," and he gestures towards a phial of alcohol, "swab that peter clean. And keep it clean until you get out of this man's army!" Humiliated, the youth turns his back, drops his clothes to the floor, and with saliva cleans his penis. I am third in line, and shielding my privates, I check my prepuce. Being totally naked is itself a nightmare, and being singled out for poor hygiene would be traumatic. I quietly rotate my fingers around my glans. The MD thumps my chest and back, examines my teeth, ears, and eyes, performs a short-arm inspection, and checks for hernias and piles. "You'll need dental work, but you'll do." He waves me on. "Next."

Still naked, I proceed in line past cages where attendants fling fatigues, OD (off-duty) brown gabardines, underwear, socks, shoes, bedding, and packs at us. One cage is devoted entirely to issuing M1 rifles. "Don't hold it by the barrel, Klutz," shouts the noncommissioned officer.

At the barracks, five minutes away, a sergeant who bellows contempt and singles out a draftee for banging his rifle against a two-by-four building support. I shiver. As we stow our gear, hurriedly make our beds (it will take me a week to manage the hospital blanket corners), the sergeant strides the long, narrow room. He orders us out for our first close-order drill. During formation I hang back, avoiding the front rows. I have only the dimmest sense of what makes a soldier. My tall, stalwart build implies that I am better coordinated than I am. We are instructed in coming to attention, saluting, and marching. The first man of each row is leader. Guys avid to be noticed struggle for position. Once we settle down I find that my mistakes are no more egregious than most made by other men. Blocked into squads, we parade for an hour.

None of us knows where he will be assigned. We are told that this stay, at Fort Sheridan outside Chicago, will be brief. "Don't think of makin' a nest here," the sergeant warns. A battery of IQ tests indicates that my verbal aptitudes qualify me for ASTP, the Army Specialized Training Corps, as a translator. My over-all score is 120. Since ASTP schooling is a guarantee that you won't end up in combat, I am anxious to go. I learn, however, that huge casualties in Europe necessitate the demise of the program. I am assigned to a rifle platoon and await orders. Men seem selected at random for new units. Friends are rarely assigned together.

Finally, after two weeks, my name appears on a roster. The cadre, the permanent staff, do not divulge where we are going. We receive platoon assignments with appointees to squad and company command positions from our own ranks. Needless to say, I am not one of those chosen, though I believe I have leadership qualities.

Waiting for the bus to the train, I am homesick. I've had only one letter from home, bearing affection but little news. I manage to write daily letters, cramming them with the minutiae of each day's events, sketching some of the men, reaffirming my love, and underscoring my faith in Jesus.

The journey south requires two nights. We sit up all the way, breathing in air befouled with cigarette smoke. I am not yet a smoker, but many men are. Earlier, when we boarded the train, solicitous American Red Cross women proffered free packages of Camels. Treacly love dripped from their plump faces as they "facilitated their boys" on to their destinies. There was no time for them to converse past asking what states we were from. For the first hours I observe landscapes and towns pass, penciling notes in a spiral book. The railroad track is an umbilical chord winding towards an unknown geography. Catching the names of hamlets as we rush through becomes a game. Later, I chart our route on a map. I record dogs running beside the train, horses and cows in pastures, waving farmers, slum apartments with greasy windows fronting the railroad yards. Eventually, there are numerous blacks.

As we approach Georgia, we assume we're headed for Fort Benning. "That's fucked," says a short, stubby Texan. "They're ain't no way they'll take us dummies for paratroops. You've got to be smart before they let you jump from airplanes."

Another voice: "Now that there's no more volunteers, draftees has to fill up the paratroops. Women will love the boots and berets."

The rumor proves false, for at dawn we creep into South Carolina. Swamps. No crocodiles. Cottony mist shrouds the cypress trees. Palmettos. Sharecropper hovels. "Coloreds Only" signs hanging off a drinking fountain and a rest room in Florence. A malnourished black brother and sister beg at our windows. I throw down chocolate bars. "Them's cute pickaninnies," says the Texan. "Give 'em a few years and they'll sprout them big asses." He clears his throat. "If you run your fingers through their hair, you'd crawl with cooties. See their filthy kinks."

Early that evening we reach Fort Jackson. An NCO informs us that we are the new 442nd Infantry, headed for combat in Europe. The insignia is a lion's head with mouth agape and protruding tongue. The NCO in charge, First Sergeant E. V. Griffin, is a forty-year old, lean Georgian, with two fingers missing from his right hand, damaged at Monte Casino. I am assigned to Sergeant Joe Lynch's Company D. Lynch, a Pacific War veteran, is short, stocky, muscular, about thirty. There is no doubt that he is in charge. Basic training will last three months.

Like most GIs I believe in the war; Hitler and Tojo are Satan incarnate. Christianity requires that Good and Evil conflict. How else can Light triumph over Dark? Images of God's smiting arm and of Old Testament variations on the ancient code of Hammurabi appeared to me first in Wisconsin where Seventh Day Adventists proffered their wretchedly printed tomes stamped in fake gold. "Armageddon is at hand!" My mother never allowed the zealots inside our house. Rebuffed, they nevertheless left literature, which I would read, amazed and troubled by the militancy of Christian armies slaughtering both heathens and one another. Every angel was vengeful. The Adventists prophesied a disastrous war with Germany. After much destruction (America would win, they believed), God would incinerate the entire planet, releasing hordes of angels with burning swords to butcher false believers.

Reading the Bible had already convinced me that I was one of the elect. I deserved His bliss. If I survived the war, I vowed to become a Lutheran minister, disseminating God's holy love. Battlefields were icy walls concealing horrific nightmares.

In a dream, centurions shove me across slimy flagstones. I wear nothing but a white linen cloth knotted diaper-fashion about by loins. A thin rear strip drawn up between my buttocks is secured at the waist. On reaching a stone lintel the centurions shove my head down. My feet slue, propelling me into a dark interior with a stench of animal fur. "Come," says a gentle voice. "I'm Daniel. Have no fear." He wears a multi-colored, striped desert robe, and stands among a pride of lions. "I'm waiting for you," he says, dropping his robe, revealing a stunning white, sturdy, almost hairless, late-adolescent body. He takes my hand, studies the palm, then holds it to his lips. "Never kill," he says, embracing me. His flesh is marble-cold. I am no longer anxious.

Chaplain Crutchfield, a pudgy man with short blond hair, wearing an immaculately pressed shirt, shuffles papers on his desk. From an ante room, hymn tones from a field organ drift. The player repeats a difficult passage, shortly jamming his fingers in frustration. Visible through the door is a portable communion altar of the sort used during maneuvers and battles. A luxuriant bouquet of lilacs adorns the altar.

I don't know whether to salute Crutchfield. Is he a true officer? The silver bars he wears says he is; the silver cross says he is not. I don't salute.

"Sir," I say, "I need your help."

He gestures towards a chair. "Don't be nervous, lad." He straightens some papers. "Now," he leans back. "What can I do for you?" Another flourish of jangling organ chords. "Wilson!" Crutchfield shouts. "Practice later, when I'm not here." He returns to me. "Sorry. The assistant's new. I'm trying him out for this Sunday."

"It's about killing," I say. "I don't know if I can kill another human."

He stares. He's examining an aura rather than living flesh. The longer he's silent the more uneasy I am.

"I've heard all this before, you know." Still, the stolid mouth, the eyes luring me without a hint of compassion. "You've been screened by the Army psychologist, right?"

"Yes," I reply, missing his drift.

"You're not goin' to cry, are you? A lot of boys come in here, crybabies baring their souls." He waits. "That's rough, I know. And it may not apply to you. You shouldn't tell me any secrets, like, if you're a queer. I'm under oath to transmit all such information to the battalion commander. These losers should have stayed home wearing dresses and baking cookies for us real men overseas. Know what I mean?" He studies me. "The U.S. jams faggots into stockades and throws dishonorable discharges at 'em."

"I plan to be a Lutheran minister," I say. "I was superintendent of the Sunday School. I believe in the Bible word for word. Jesus said to turn the other cheek. He commanded us not to kill." Clearly, the chaplain, I knew, would misread my dream of Daniel.

"Well, there's no room in this Army for perverts. Once they've gotten past the psychiatrists, us chaplains have to ferret them out. You're not one, are you?"

"Explain the commandment *not to kill!*"

"Look, Bob, it's Bob, right? I'm a life-long Presbyterian, and I don't have a problem at all. Just do what your NCO's and officers say. That's your job." He's vexed. "Jump when they say. Shoot when they say. They're responsible. It's between them and God. Got that? There's lots of gardenias in the world to sniff, but there's tons of shit too, both animal and human." He rises, dismissing me. "Might help if you come to services Sunday. They're interdenominational. Should be something there for you to grab onto."

I lick my wounds. I do not then realize how friable my faith is, nor how naive I am. Yet, Jesus's roseate glow remains pacifist; the Israelite code is militant with prejudice and butchery. A few men in Company D read books. Joe Beck loved Gertrude Stein, and since I had memorized portions of *Ida* in high school, we talked a good line. Actually, I was not an efficient reader, starting numerous books without finishing them. My hunger to write was a craving rather than something I was disciplined and skilled enough to execute. Having been named after Robert Louis Stevenson (i.e., *Robert Louis Peters*) I trusted that I had the famous author's writing genes.

In the unit, pecking orders soon jelled. While I never played lackey, I spread obeisance before anyone potentially hostile. I might discover, for example, that powerful, macho Ross Brown came from Minnesota. I would buddy up by pretending to like fishing for muskie and walleyed pike. When I realized that inveterate gambler Ben Throck loved an appreciative audience, I hovered at his elbow, admiring the way he shouted out his cards. The balance, was, as they say, "nice." No one seemed threatened by me, nor suspicious that my buddying had sexual overtones. To thrust your hand in horse play between the nates of a well-formed male most men considered healthy. Any hint of romantic involvement, though, raised danger flags. Soft, affectionate voices were for women; tough, vibrant voices, though caring, must never undercut our male bravado.

Daily life levelled most pretensions. Someone was always within arm's reach, even at night. To feel the leg of a man in the next bed thrash suddenly toward yours was common. The latrines reduced you immediately to the lowest common denominator. The urinals, porcelain or galvanized metal receptacles attached to a wall, were arranged so that men stood shoulder to shoulder, emitting golden streams. As for the stools, none had partitions: imagine sitting with a dozen defecating men, knees almost touching, with shorts or trousers bunched around your ankles. You squatted amidst this olio of attars and anal plosives, unless, of course, you were particularly sensitive and held it in until two in the morning, when everyone else was asleep. We rarely gazed at men at stool or urinal. And footlockers were sacrosanct. To steal was heinous.

Curiously, there was little nudity. Few men loved parading themselves. In fact, the appropriate garb, even on the hottest days, were generic, sexless, olive-drab boxer shorts. One exception was Gene Burkey, possessor of the largest cock in the company. When we asked him to flip the monster forth, it proved one of those tools exactly the same size either flaccid or hard. For laughs he would daub on shoe polish to simulate eyes and brows, calling the result "Mary Sunshine."

Most men were meticulously clean. One who was not was "Poontang," a rural Midwesterner of immense pinkish hue, soft lips which always hung wetly open, and marginal mentality. He seldom showered, and when he grew too noisome the barracks bathed him. After lights out, four men dragged him to the showers, forced him to soap himself, and then proceeded to scrub him with latrine brushes. He screamed, and when they stopped, his arms, chest, and thighs were bloody. After that, he showered daily.

Homosexuality was always joked about, derided, and condemned. There was talk of sodomy ("cornholing" was the term). Guys endowed with well-sculpted asses were told that if they wore a wig and trimmed hair from their legs and nates, they'd be good pussy. An attractive platoon sergeant in the next company was gossiped about merely because he had an androgynous face and a small penis barely visible in a nest of black hair. A scandal occurred when an older GI named Wisher erected a pup tent near the base and began spending his nights in the field.

21

Sergeant Lynch, suspicious, surprised him engaged in fellatio with a platoon sergeant. Both men were placed under armed guard and shipped to a stockade. Lynch addressed the company: "You know the penalty for putting another man's cock in your mouth?" He scrutinized us. "You rot in prison for life. You'll get fucked good there." Several times that week I walked to the spot where the pup tent had stood, lingering in a mix of fear and awe. I had liked Wisher. He was a technician for Broadway plays, and gave me my first glimpses into that rare world.

Among the protocols I failed to manage were salutes. Despite my having practiced in mirrors, my efforts were wretched. I had been reprimanded at Fort Sheridan, where a sergeant drilled me, thinking, finally, that he had won, that I had learned from him exactly how the index and adjoining fingers were to be brought together, deftly touching the right eyebrow before being tossed smartly forward in a snap, the palm of the hand never facing the receiver of the salute. To this day, I relive this failure, and at war films loathe those smart snappers born to salute.

I had other failures. During basic training, those of us who were literate (many draftees could barely read or write) were expected to keep notes of lectures and demonstrations, held usually on gravel areas and hillocks, conducted by the lieutenants and the NCOs. I hated drills in plane identification, and never learned to distinguish an Allied plane from a Nazi one unless it carried a visible Baltic Cross.

We were repeatedly informed that our "piece," our M1 rifle, was dearer to us than any person living or dead; we should, therefore, treat it accordingly. Though I spent much time polishing and oiling it, and felt pride and trust, I feared squeezing the trigger. Moreover, I was the slowest soldier in the platoon at dismantling the gun, and I never learned the names of the parts, despite making lists and reciting the names before going to sleep. The platoon sergeant concluded that anyone so inept wouldn't last long in combat, so why should he worry—I'd just get my ass shot off.

Nor was I any better at the manual of arms, that synchronized ballet where you swing the rifle through various patterns from parade rest to landing the stock on your right shoulder, bringing the piece in a smart diagonal across your body and with a swift, deft thrust of the thumb opening the breech and presenting the gun to your inspecting officer, who peers down the barrel, looking for a slick, grit-free interior.

My most shocking failure occurred during a battalion retreat. Each

22

of the four regiments were assembled, with Company D to the left of Company C, and so on. Our regiment, alas, was directly in the commander's primary line of view. When the time came for the manual of arms, I alone was out of sync.

"Who's that soldier?" bellowed the major. "Order him here at once."

"Sir," I snapped one of my peculiar salutes.

"Who taught you your manual of arms, boy?"

Silence.

"Sergeant? Are you responsible?"

Sergeant Griffin saluted. "Yes, Sir."

"Well, he's a disgrace. Stay with him, night and day, until he masters the drill. Is that clear, Sergeant?"

"Yes, Sir." Then Griffin turned to Sergeant Lynch. "Lynch," he bellowed, "drill this fruit until he's learned how to throw a rifle better than anyone in the company."

Lynch ordered me to an empty barracks room where, after several frustrating sessions, he gave up, advising me either to miss all future retreats or stay to the rear, invisible.

My primary task—D Squad was the mortar platoon—was to carry the mortar base plate on which more adept soldiers would mount the barrel and fire the weapon. Even the ammo bearers felt superior to plate-toters. Like so much else in the army, the piece was olive drab. Once secured to your shoulders by a strip of webbing, it projected six inches or so from either side. In addition, you carried a rifle, a pack, a gas mask, and a canteen.

Target practice was another frustration. Although the NCO coached me to "squeeze" the trigger, I always flinched, fearing the recoil. I earned numerous "Maggie's Drawers." My ineptitude with guns dated from the farm, when the best I managed with a .22 rifle was to spray the dirt behind a squirrel or to maim a bumblebee deep inside a morning glory where it was sipping nectar. I perpetually let my squad down. I also failed to climb hand over hand up a rope during obstacle course training.

Bill Seltzer, from St. Louis, promised to help me master the ropes, and for several evenings I struggled. Bill's lithe body was perfectly suited for calisthenics. He had developed strong upper arms, and held his body erect, as though prepared to flash off on a run or scurry up a rope. He wanted to be a wrestling coach, he said. While I matched him in chin-ups and push-ups, I never succeeded in the hand-over-hand

23

climb. When I asked Bill if my body was wrong, too chunky perhaps, he said: "No. It's all in the timing. Be a puma. Let yourself go." No matter how puma-like I felt, I never could propel myself up that dismal rope.

I loved long marches and saw them as a persistence of will, proving my mettle. I recall one humid thirty-miler, much of it over baking blacktop which cut through palmetto and pine forests, leading to several miles of sandy roads. We were limited to a canteen of water apiece.

At a rest stop in a woods, we were ordered to excavate two-man foxholes, camouflaging them with scrub oak branches, simulating an "enemy" lobbing mortar shells our way. My partner was Butch McFadden, a lanky saturnine Irishman with a peeling, sunburned face and sandy hair. Though we were exhausted from hiking, much of it over heat-softened tar, we dug a good foxhole. All the while McFadden bitched. As the only son of an aging father, he should have been deferred, he felt, to manage the family hardware store. Moreover, he had married his high school sweetheart just prior to being drafted. "This shit was never meant for me," he'd say, throwing his trenching spade against a tree. He mastered the fine line between lagging too far behind and lagging just enough, bugging the NCO. That evening Butch plucked wild asters, stuck them around the rim of the hole, and sat hunkered, smoking a cigarette. "Not a bad sunset," he observed. "Though I'd much rather be watchin' it in Nebraska."

"I'm going to get some sleep," I said. "It's a long hike back."

"Good idea," said McFadden, joining me.

I was awakened by his pumping against my back. "Some dream" he said with a sheepish look. "I soaked myself." He climbed up to the surface, stripped off his trousers and shorts, and wiped himself with the latter, which he rolled into a ball and stuffed into his pack. "I thought you were my horny wife," he grinned.

I leave McFadden and walk through a grove of scrub pines to a small palmetto-fringed lake with milky turquoise water. Almost a perfect circle, the lake has a surround of golden sand some two feet wide which protects the water from encroaching shrubs and weeds. There are neither bird nor animal tracks. The lake itself is free of sedge and water plants. The sun rays melting west add to the luminescence.

Most lakes are the eyes of God, the circumference inviting you to swim through time. Hushed, reverent, I cross the sand which I find loose, my feet sinking in to the ankles. Near the glinting turquoise water, I draw off my shoes, then my clothes. I inhale, throw back my chest, my arms at my sides. Thunder rumbles like a gong struck with a wool-covered hammer. I kneel, immersing my hands. The water, with the viscosity of warm blood, must be logged with salts. I bend over, as a primitive might, with my head forward, my arms up to the elbows. An odor of mustard sweetened with mint. Veins dangle from my chest, arms, and loins. No voice speaks, nor do I feel a need to swallow water, to anoint my face, or to plunge in.

How long I remain on the shore I don't recall. There's a command to resume marching. A full moon shimmers. On the way back, I join in the marching songs. We reach the barracks shortly after midnight.

Even today, the turquoise lake recurs in dreams. If the vision occurs during stress, I am restored. A dozen years ago I drove to South Carolina seeking the lake, but failed to find it. Had it existed?

On bivouacs, since each of us carried half a tent, we required a partner. Mine was Arthur Crook, a lanky North Carolinian who chewed tobacco, spoke in a broad southern drawl, was barely literate, sang hillbilly songs, and played a five-string banjo and jew's harp. Too inept, like me, to affix a mortar tube to its base, or set an azimuth and drop in mortar shells, Crook was doomed to lugging mortar base plates.

Crook joked about his big feet, consciously tripping over them. He was so adept at spitting tobacco we'd set up targets and lay bets on whether he'd hit them; he always did. He was never without a plug in his cheek. He seldom stood totally erect. His walk, crab-like, was his own. When an officer ordered him to attention, he'd salute smartly, chuck the tobacco wad further into his cheek, and give a disarming smile. He was a free spirit who believed that our friendship was eternal.

Except on separate work details, we were together. Whenever Crook was delayed, I never went to bed until he appeared. No one brushed his teeth as often as Crook, and he washed his hair daily in his helmet. He kept his banjo inside a blue canvas bag. I felt very masculine around him.

Eventually, in England, he was sent to an infantry company destined for Omaha Beach. Since he never wrote letters, my letters to him during and after the war were never answered.

25

While on maneuvers in Tennessee, Captain Porter, the commanding officer, named me his runner. Porter was a slender army career man in his late forties whose cheekbones resembled steel plates thrust beneath his skin. I ran messages from him to other commanders on the fringes of our mock war. I delivered most of them orally so that if the "enemy" captured me there'd be no written evidence. With my M1 slung over my shoulder, I would dash through scrub, imagining Germans on the adjacent hills. The company depended on my getting through. I imitated Indian scouts from movies: planting a heel first enabled me to avoid snapping twigs.

I loved Porter's war games. I would find him poised on an "Observation Point" facing the "enemy," wearing his helmet, pistol in holster, binoculars in hand, consulting with some NCO. I would salute (I seemed to be getting better) and say "Scout reporting, Sir." My report made, I lingered nearby until it was time for another run.

On these maneuvers, simulated battle conditions required a careful posting of guards from dusk to dawn. All men pulled these duties. The challenge: "Who goes there? Advance and be recognized." The capture: if the enemy captured you, you gave only your name, rank, and serial number. You paced the perimeters listening for suspicious night sounds, particularly for "hostile troops" launching a raid. Always alert, you cocked your rifle, and, if necessary, sounded an alarm (a whistle carried around your neck).

One of my watch details transpired during an enormous hoarfrost, under a brilliant moon. Behind the mess hall were boxes of ice-cold oranges, some covered with rime, which I raided, eating many as fast as I could.

Captain Porter announced that he was modifying reveille. Since a simple bugle call was not enough, he was adding a bass drum, which I would pound. At 4:45 each morning the bugler and I would march, rousing the troops.

"You'll learn fast," said the captain with his usual ebullience. "I'll teach you myself."

After an hour of intensive instruction, he pronounced me fit. "Tomorrow I'll hear you loud and clear," he said.

My barracks mates scoffed at my cadences, saying I should pound for burlesque houses. The bugler was annoyed, preferring, as he always had, to stand in one place for reveille. "This is a bunch of shit," he declared through his red lips, jerking my drum as though he'd smash it.

26

After a month the captain ordered me to attend barber's school. "In life you have to go from one thing to the next," he said. "Return your drum to the supply sergeant." I would be placed on temporary duty, excused from regular training.

The regimental barber shop had six chairs, was operated by a cadre of veterans on limited duty because of war injuries, and used no electricity. Since we were training for battle, the logic went, we should cut hair under simulated field conditions. I never quite caught the rhythm of comb and scissors. When I slashed too much hair, the soldier was outraged. When I cut too little he felt cheated. When the master barber saw a crude swath he could usually repair the damage. We spent fifteen minutes per scalp. Fortunately, the cuts were free.

Seated behind his desk, Captain Porter flipped a bed sheet at me. "Here, Peters. I need a trim." He produced a scissors, then called the first sergeant over. "See what your men are in for, Sergeant Griffin."

I trimmed gingerly. His chestnut hair had an odd fineness, almost like a girl's. He asked for a mirror. "Not too bad," he said. "You're now the official company barber." Most of my "customers" (or "victims," depending on your point of view) were men either the first sergeant or Captain Porter had singled out as sartorially negligent.

Like my playing bass drum, barbering too ran its course. My next assignment was with the regimental newspaper, *The Fighter*. In addition to ferreting out human interest stories—anecdotes of events on base, news of marriages and births, and jokes—I wrote an interview column and would trip about the regiment asking questions: "What is your favorite movie? Sport? What will you do when the war is over?" We never ran items on national or world affairs, and made no attempt to inform the troops as to the progress of the war. The officer in charge, Lt. Bernie Kaplan, an avid Philadelphia journalist and a slender, nattily-dressed man, used the paper to glorify the regiment and to assist his own promotion to higher echelons. The values, as he saw them, were to preserve the history of the unit, to instill pride in the regiment, and to maintain morale. We named many soldiers per issue and encouraged them to send the paper home. From Kaplan I learned the value of terseness and economy in writing, how to see the salient point in a story, and how to do lay-outs and paste-ups.

By mid-November, on our maneuvers near Murphreesboro, Tennessee, I was editor, with a staff of two—a young artist from the Pennsylvania mountains, and a writer from Chicago. We set up in a second floor print shop on the town's main square, courtesy of the owner, "Happy" Trevathan, an old-time printer. Lieutenant Kaplan had a jeep for our use. During the night we slept on the print shop floor, the officer keeping his distance across the room. His faith in *The Fighter*, he stressed, was not shared by the regimental commander who felt that the army would be better served if we were in the field. Because of the lieutenant's connections, the paper continued until he was transferred elsewhere. On the rare occasions I rejoined my regular unit, I was teased for joining "queers and fairies."

My closest friends now, all in the mortar platoon, were Arthur Sheppi; Bill Seltzer, my calisthenics pal; Jim Blackie, a tall, stooped youth from Joliet, Illinois, who served time in reform school for burglary; Joe Lattal, a sturdy guy from Chicago with a robust, Rabelaisian humor; Bob Becker, the Californian interested in writing novels; and Jeff Root, a flashy womanizer from Baltimore.

It was Becker who wrote the imitations of Gertrude Stein, which he read aloud to me. Stein gave us license to jot down whatever came into our heads. I loved her puns—she named a poodle "Love" because he was blind. My one effort at a novel, made well before I knew of Stein, was conventional. My subject was the German slaughter of the entire population of the Czech town of Lidice in reprisal for the assassination of a Nazi official. I wanted *Lidice* to be "beautiful," so I acquired a wallpaper sample book from the local hardware store and scrawled my saga across its pages, eschewing those designs too dark to make for easy reading. Kneeling on my attic bedroom floor, I filled nearly fifty pages. A quill pen completed my romantic writer's posture. I had no protagonist, no sense of place, and wrote dialogue of an amazing insensitivity. I began in *media res* by focusing on a mother holding a baby in her lap, amidst villagers already slaughtered by the Nazis. When she pleads for her baby's life, a German smashes her face with a rifle butt. Another German grabs the child and spears it, holding it aloft as in anti-Nazi propaganda posters.

Despite these feeble efforts, I realized that a writer must treat encompassing themes, preferably ones detailing man's inhumanity to man and his triumph. If I had created a young Czech survivor who avenges his village, I might have unified my book and even finished it.

Like other GIs I drank much beer at the PX, attended films, and occasionally travelled by bus to Columbia for an evening of dancing and ogling women. We saw movies before they were released to civilians. My favorites starred Alice Faye, Carmen Miranda, Rita Hayworth, and Marlene Dietrich. These actresses, even when overtly sexual, like Dietrich and Hayworth, remained curiously chaste. Below the neck they were manikins draped in some of the most gorgeous gowns ever designed, packaged like primary orchids glowing among lesser ones, to be admired rather than possessed. Though a cusp of luscious buttock glimmered through the lamé, and the turn of the ample thigh seemed to invite tongue and finger strokes, these stars were sanitized by their fashion-plate style.

I romanticized these actresses. Dietrich's luscious skin, the satiny drooping lids, the moist lips, the husky voice, all induced ecstasy. While Hayworth was exotic, her sexual pirouettes were choreographed dance movements, not entire love feasts. She was always clothed, and in that great scene in *Gilda* where she removes her gloves for Glen Ford she is an archetypal sexual tease, as pure and cold as marble. During the forties, the phrase "sex Goddess" meant something now lost—the female idealized yet tantalizingly real, finally inaccessible, to be adored as goddesses always have been, sans sweat glands, sans pubic hairs, sans food in their teeth. Carmen Miranda, like the comedienne Virginia O'Brien, parodied these women. I also adored the Andrews Sisters and Martha Raye.

On weekends we wandered Columbia, admiring the great, columned, antebellum mansions, and lingering on the fringes of the black slums. While I found the "coloreds only" signs vaguely offensive, I accepted them as integral to Southern culture. Growing up in northern Wisconsin, where a black face was seldom seen, I had never confronted prejudice. In the early thirties a middle-aged black couple, the McCarthys, lived in Eagle River. Why they chose to live there I never knew. He was ample-girthed and might have passed for white; she, short and slender, had kinky graying hair. McCarthy was an accomplished banjo player, and he and Dad spent evenings together, either at our house or theirs, playing music. I never felt that the McCarthys were inferior. The region, though, because of the summer influx of Jews from Chicago and Milwaukee, was thoroughly anti-Semitic.

As a draftee assigned to an all-white infantry regiment constituted of the least-educated, poorest recruits in the nation, I absorbed anti-black prejudices. My images came from films: Step-n-Fetchit was the archetypal blubber-lipped, shiftless black so lazy he could hardly speak. Even as charismatic an athlete, actor, and singer as Paul Robeson was demeaned in *Show Boat*. I felt that drinking from "white" public fountains and using "whites only" rest rooms guaranteed that we would avoid "black" diseases. And wasn't poverty evidence of inferiority? In a country of unlimited opportunities like America, if you failed, the fault was yours. The presence of a black lieutenant-general, Benjamin Davis, in the military hierarchy seemed an anomaly; the officer had merely proved himself "white."

My most intimate experience with blacks came during maneuvers. I had been riding in *The Fighter*'s jeep. We hit mud. The jeep mired. There was no way to free it without a truck. Our feet were frozen. The lieutenant noticed a log cabin and suggested we go there to wait for a passing GI truck.

An aged black woman with gray frizzed hair opened the door to a dark interior lighted by a single window covered with oiled paper. She welcomed us to her charred stone fireplace, the only source of warmth. The heat, though dim, was sustaining.

I was shocked by the poverty. Torn pages of old, fly-specked newspapers and magazines covered the bare walls. A much-abused kitchen table and three chairs sat near the fire. A single board shelf held old crockery and pans. The floor was entirely of earth. I couldn't understand a word the woman said, and she coughed much, perpetually smiling, showing decayed teeth. "She wants to serve coffee," the officer said, pointing to an old granite pot sitting on a fireplace ledge. The coffee, largely chicory, was thick and scalding. There was no milk.

I did not then see the obvious connections between her house and the house I had grown up in: plank floors, bare log walls and studs, nail ends poking through the cheap roof tar paper, newspaper pasted up as insulation against the cold, a plain cast-iron stove for both heating and cooking, images of cows cut from condensed milk cans and pasted by my mother to her kitchen cupboard doors.

As basic training concluded, I worried about departing overseas. Most of my time was spent on special duty assignments, ill-preparing me for infantry combat. There seemed no way of changing my military occupation specialty to anything other than rifleman.

In February of 1943 rumors spread that we were going to England. We preferred Europe to Asia, for the Japanese were reputedly more vicious than the Germans. Each platoon, company, and regiment now had leaders from their own ranks. The cadre, including Griffin and Lynch, would stay behind to train the raw troops replacing us.

We were granted ten-day furloughs. My family was living then in Sawyer, Wisconsin, in Door Country, within easy driving distance of the Sturgeon Bay shipyard where Dad was a welder. I hitchhiked the last twenty miles through cherry orchards and arrived home. Dad was in a good mood, happy to be contributing to "the home front line of industry." Ironically, he later developed stomach cancer from the lead fumes he ingested.

The return to Ft. Jackson was smooth. I travelled alone, my papers within easy reach. Seeing the men I had lived and trained with for so many weeks was more like a homecoming than the actual furlough had been. The sadness? We would shortly separate, on our way to combat, we supposed.

I recall the morning of our departure. Wearing full battle gear, we lay on our stripped bunks with rolled packs waiting for orders to move out. The company clerk appeared—he was part of the permanent cadre, so would not be going to Europe. "Peters, I've changed your MOS," he said, "to clerk typist."

He had scrutinized my records, he explained, including my performances on the rifle range, and, on his own, decided that the change was fair. He hoped I was pleased. I thanked him effusively.

"Well, you'd better go back," he said. "You'll be called shortly."

He probably saved my life. While I can see his face most clearly, I can't recall his name.

3

England:
April 1944–October 1944

I N T H E troop ship leaving Boston, a former luxury liner converted
for transporting GIs, we are billeted deep in incredibly cramped
quarters. We feel oddly legless as the harbor swells, lifting and
resettling the ship. Although huge engines circulate air, the hold is
rancid with cigarette smoke and body odor. Mae West life jackets will
protect us if we are torpedoed. We wear the jackets even when we
sleep.

There are perpetual crap and poker games, none of which I join. I
have never understood gambling, though I love playing cards—500
rummy, pinochle, and smear. Having grown up with little cash, I dread
losing what I have and never feel lucky. Most of my meager pay I invest
in Savings Bonds, to be waiting when the war ends.

Films are shown in the mess area. And for the first time we receive those marvelous paper books published for service men. These
are three inches by five, and vary greatly in subject. I prefer history
and biography to fiction. Louis Untermeyer's poetry collections are
included.

We sail via Greenland and Iceland, our route zigzagging as a way of
confusing German U-boats. I never understand the strategy. Won't a
submarine spot us despite the camouflage paint and z-shaped route?
Near Greenland (I never see it; we pass by night) we join a convoy of
supply ships. Though our vessel is the most visible, the other ships will
provide safety. Also, submarines patrol our flanks. If we are sunk, survivors will be rescued.

Whenever the ship gives a violent thud, it drops into a trough, rolling on its side before righting itself. I tilt instinctively against the roll, as

though my puny effort at ballast will help. When someone claims to spot a periscope, apprehensions are almost palpable. On quiet nights I love standing near the keel, tracing the wake, its phosphorescence producing an acute sense of distance traversed. I ache for home: kitchen odors, resinous pine blazing in the living room heater, fresh milk striking a pail, and even the rancid smells of the hen house. I crave letters from Mom. Dad rarely writes, self-conscious as he is about his spelling. In his whole life he probably writes a dozen letters, no more.

Daily routines ease our boredom: calisthenics, lectures on Britain, training films, anti-Hun and big-toothed Japanese propaganda movies, and assorted work details. We scrub decks, mess areas, and latrines. We pull guard duty. There is little or no fraternization with the sailors; an unwritten code says that the services must ignore one another.

Indoctrination on the British is intense. They are a proud people, so we are told, so don't act superior—although we are again forced to save them from the Germans, as we did in World War I. Don't call them "Limeys" or ridicule their tea. Their monetary system is quirky. English women have body odor (which they spell "odour") and rotten teeth. English girls love candy ("sweets") and black Americans, so don't shout obscenities when you see women pushing half-caste babies in prams. English beer is warm (don't compare it to piss), and you must observe their rigid pub closing times. Honor their queues. They queue for cinemas, ration books, and fish and chips. They have a powerful sense of fair play and think Yanks are pushy. So, if you are at the back of a line, stay there. Remember, we're allies, not an occupation force. Most of you will go directly to staging areas for France, Belgium, or Holland. Some of you will assault the beaches. Expect to see English cities blitzed to smithereens by German bombs. Though the Great Blitz ended in 1940, the Luftwaffe continues the destruction.

Early evening. Smoke and flames on the horizon. Two days out from England. A ship explodes. Power on our ship dies. We are ordered below. Then, before panic ensues, the massive engines catch and the lights return. Shortly, over the intercom system, the CO informs us that while we have lost a ship, the men are rescued and the U-boat sunk. By daylight, a massive oil-slick crests with the rollers, blackening our ship. Bits of flotsam slue and slide, washing past us.

At 10:00 A.M. on the eighth day after leaving Boston, in a fog so thick we can't see the quay until we dock, we reach Southampton. Women in flimsy floral dresses, drab jackets, and hats with floppy brims blow kisses. We toss cigarettes, gum, and candy. Aged policemen are on watch. There's a cadre of British air force men. The pier itself is a vast decaying warehouse with pigeon guano smearing beams and pilings. A solitary Union Jack hangs over the entrance to a debarkation hall from which we proceed to a convoy of camouflaged U.S. Army trucks ready to start for the west of England—just where, we are not told. We vie for rear seats, the better to see the towns and countryside. As we rumble through villages, our trucks reverberate with ear-shattering force. The countryside is incredible—vast meadows of an almost fiery green, huge sweeping oaks and plane trees, herds of fat grazing sheep and cows, thatched roofs, and roses like gigantic peonies. The greens of Wisconsin pale in comparison. Most houses have vegetable, or "victory," gardens. Vacant spaces near railroad tracks and in empty fields and allotments, each marked by wire fences and wooden palings, are crammed with vegetables, part of the national movement to increase the food supply. If there is an odor special to the country, it rises from the diesel fuel spewing black clouds from lorries wheeling through the streets and along the narrow highways, and from the pungent coal burned in factories and in homes.

We arrive at Warminster, in Wiltshire, roughly sixty-five miles northwest of Southampton, much nearer to Salisbury, and only eight miles from Stonehenge. Bath, the ancient spa city, and Bristol, which is badly bombed, are also nearby.

On the outskirts of Warminster, nestled in a long valley between largely treeless rolling hills, is a vast military base. By our standards, the base is flimsy. The single-story barracks are made of thin wood covered with tar paper. They are squat, built to accommodate short men. Anyone over six feet brushes the rafters. The hodge-podge arrangement of buildings lacks the meticulous logic of American bases. The whole place is treeless.

Lend Lease—Roosevelt's program to assist the money-strapped British by loaning them military equipment—requires that we utilize English food and materials. In our barracks, for example, are double-decker, bare-wire beds and empty mattress ticking that we stuff with straw from a community pile. We complain. We complain also about the bread, and crave the squishy white stuff so indigenous to the American diet. British bread tastes of sawdust. We believe, in fact, that sawdust is the primary ingredient; for aren't the Germans similarly extending meager wheat supplies? We are served this weighty, brown (and nutritious) bread in slabs rather than slices. Then, powdered eggs! Every dawn in the dim mess hall we smother the foul eggs in catsup, the bread in peanut butter and jam. The coffee is notoriously bad, mostly chicory. I develop a tolerance for the eggs, which, when mixed with milk and scrambled in butter, are palatable, although a metallic taste, laced with mustard, persists.

We settle into a routine of early morning calisthenics, training lectures, and hikes over the downs. No roads have markers; for the British, fearing a German invasion, have removed all signs. Ancient stiles are stowed for the duration. It seems obvious that the Germans will invade Britain, probably near the Isle of Wight. So many GIs are assembled in camps along the eastern coast we joke that England will tip into the sea, leaving behind a litter of helmet liners, field packs, K-rations, condoms, and gas masks. I can imagine the horror of racing, rifle in hand, across a beach towards German cannons and machine guns. I am part of a vast charade. God will bring me home.

We have almost daily bayonet practice, using human-looking bundles of straw clad in captured Nazi uniforms that are set up in a field. On command, with bayonets drawn, we lunge, emitting bloodcurdling screams, ramming our blades through the Germans. Straw Germans can't retaliate.

One hike takes us to Stonehenge. Isolated in a field near Amesbury, it looks stark and brooding in the mist. I have only vague notions of what I am seeing, having remembered the stones from a *National Geographic*. Archaeologists assume that Druids erected the craggy columns for observing the solstices. The air seems redolent with blood. Facing a massive lintel, I am stirred by the beauty. The size of the boulders guarantees that most will never be pulled down, crushed, and used for buildings, or buried. Nevertheless, in their isolation, they seem vulnerable. Why has no great city sprung up around them, no religious or cultural center? Why wasn't Salisbury cathedral, a few miles away, built here?

Back in camp, in clear nights, we observe clusters of Nazi bombers on missions to pulverize Bristol, Birmingham, Manchester, and Coventry. Though under severe restrictions to conceal our lights, we are still visible; Nazi intelligence must know our location. Lying in my bunk, I flinch as German planes flying over. Bristol is demolished, and flak from British ground batteries blaze. On occasion, Nazi planes drop bombs near Warminster. One explodes nearby. By three a.m. the skies are clear. Only then do we sleep.

As we draw nearer to actual war, a feeling recurs—and it is probably one, much intensified, that victims of bombings feel—that I am staked to the ground. As the bombs drop I struggle and scream. Every day now, squadrons of Allied planes fly towards German cities, preparing for an invasion. Hamburg is incinerated. With each passing week, the possibility of a German attack diminishes. As D-day nears, camp discipline, already severe, intensifies.

Despite the grimness, there are respites—strolls over the hills either alone or with friends, particularly during the long mid-summer nights when darkness falls at midnight. One particular climb provides a panoramic view of the base, the town, and on clear days of Bristol and the Wash.

I am assigned to depot headquarters as a clerk typist. The appointment is temporary; I expect to join an infantry unit destined for France. So each day is a gift, a reprieve from battle duty; and I never complain as I type boring lists of names and serial numbers of men passing on to the war front. I spend off-duty hours touch-typing numbers. I become the fastest typist in the pool. I hope to stay at headquarters.

We use incredibly tinny British typewriters, Barlocks, which are to American Underwoods as Model T Fords are to Cadillacs. Their platens seem made of congealed sand, not rubber—yet another instance of British ingenuity at compensating for scarce materials.

While I remember the barracks occupied by the typing pool, and the exact position of my typewriter on its metal desk halfway down a line of similar desks, and the row of multi-paned windows all designed in typical British rectangles, I have forgotten most of the men who worked there. The CO I do remember. He is bald, plump, in his forties, and has a huge rump clothed in those flesh-tinted gabardines worn by officers. He exudes a noisome odor, not so much of arm-pit stench but of what we jokingly call "crotch-rot." A heart murmur—that at least is the story—keeps him from a field command. Most officers in the Adjutant Generals' Department are suspected of either pulling strings or of faking health problems.

The only typist I recall, John Speak, from Charleston, South Carolina, is a husky blond with over-sized ears and the thickest of southern accents, who trained also at Ft. Jackson, specializing there in firing mortars. He was an insurance clerk before being drafted. He loves describing sex positions, which both excites and repels me. I never understand why he finds me so naive.

"You sure are a stiff one, Peters," he laughs. "Coming off the farm you should know more. When the animals and birds are a-fuckin', do you look at the trees?"

He describes the "little boat" women have. "You'll feel it when they're hot. It's like a little dick standing up in there. They love it when you rub it."

We are cautioned against divulging any military news to the British. Never trust civilians, particularly women, we are warned. Spies lurk everywhere. The best course? Keep to yourselves.

The only Englishman I regularly see is a meek barber in his fifties who rides a black bicycle, his barber tools in a bag slung over the handlebars. On rainy days—and they are numerous—he wears a soiled brown canvas overcoat, ubiquitous to men his age (as are the sturdy dark bicycles). His haircuts are ordeals, for he is not allowed to use electricity. He works in a tiny room that includes one non-adjustable barber chair and two kitchen chairs for waiting customers. Instead of a barber's smock he wears a much-frayed brown tweed jacket. He engages us in superficial pleasantries, but never discusses the war, his private history, or our lives. He'd lose his job if he were not circumspect. I give him cigarettes, which makes him nervous. Saying "Cheerio," he slips the Camels inside a vest pocket. We pay him a shilling, a quarter in American terms, per haircut, so the smokes are a bonus which he can barter. British rationing is severe.

We throng the local pubs. Most evenings there is scarcely any room inside for the regulars. The few watery-eyed old men, some of them with canes within reach, who manage seats smoke pale cigarettes and gaze at us as though we are from Mars. They seldom accommodate us, and, in fact, arrange to sit so that they won't have to speak. And we ignore them as we boisterously quaff pints of their warm beer. The proprietors, usually men too old for service, or anile women, like our money but resent us.

At the sacrosanct closing time for pubs, 10:00 P.M., we delay drinking, putting the owners in a frenzy. Arrogant, forceful, and noisy, we do all we can to subvert the rules.

Like most GIs, I drink fast, believing that tepid ale can't be lethal. I love the musty molasses taste, especially of Guinness, or "muskrat piss," as we call it. My lips eventually numb. In a small rear garden I spread-eagle on the grass as the earth spins, rotating me through its vast diurnal flow.

A hum of voices. Passing lorries. A lime tree. A scattering of white daisies peeping through thick turf. Someone strokes my hand.

"You like that, don't you?" It's Roland Stephan, a tall, gangly, almost albino corporal who perpetually smiles.

I wait.

"So, you're not talking tonight? OK. I'm patient."

Propping himself on his elbow, Stephan stares into my face. "You're asking for trouble," he teases. "Your message is 'Come take me.' "

"Don't," I say, facing him.

"You can't fool me, Peters. You can't pretend I'm not here."

"No," I say again.

He brushes hair from my face.

His smile irritates me. I want to stretch his very carmine lips into a smirk. "Don't," I insist, looking around.

"A little sign of affection, a touch here, a touch there . . . "

His tone is more educated than queer.

"I'm not queer," I declare, sitting up.

"I know what jiggles your tits, Peters. I've been around. I've seen them straight off the farm smelling of cow shit. They're ready to play. In the right light they show true colors. So, don't hide from me, Mary. It'll be our secret. Nobody need guess." He laughs. "I love the Army! I can almost taste the cum as I mozey through the barracks, especially just before reveille, after all those whipped off batches of the night." He rises, arching his eyebrows. "I'll let you off this time, but be warned, I'll be back." He blows me a kiss, then walks away.

The only homosexual I had earlier known well was Roy Kamen, a stocky senior at Wausau High School. Craggily handsome, he wore his black hair swept up and back in a pompadour. He effused an outrageous humor. His general demeanor, while masculine, had a touch of the drag-queen. We met often at the home of a mutual friend, a woman in her thirties with whom we danced to records nearly every night. Roy and Sue dipped and whirled to Fats Domino, Glen Miller, the Dorseys, the Ink Spots, Harry James, and the Andrews Sisters. During the intervals, they snuggled on a couch, smooching and caressing. Eventually, they drew me into dancing. Roy rather than Sue actually taught me, he taking the lead.

When Roy proposed that we crash the junior prom, I took it as a lark. He wore an outrageous virginal dress with a crown of cloth violets, white gloves, and a train. Before we had taken more than a couple of spins around the floor, we sensed that the chaperons were punitive. We left, finishing the night dancing at Sue's. Roy said he loved me. "No," I said. "Don't say that."

Over the next weeks, Stephan and I continue our pub conversations. One night, there is a threat of rain, with one of those English skies filled with clouds whipping in from the sea. The air is an odd mix of the sultry and the cold. Raucous voices drift from the pub, which, as usual, is jammed.

I quaff a pint and make my way to the lawn. I expect Stephan. Minutes drag. The clouds spin further east, opening the sky for a brilliant, salmon-hued display of evening dazzle. I turn over, cradling my head in my arms, and continue waiting. I am about to return to the barracks.

"Where were you?" I demand, as Roland approaches.

"We had a date?"

He sits cross-legged on the grass.

"I expected you," I say, despising my petulance.

"Well, that's more interest than you've shown so far. Come to Bath with me this weekend. You'll be safe." He laughs. "I hope the Red Cross hostel there is better than the NAAFI one."

NAAFI canteens, the British equivalents of American Red Cross or United Service Organization (USO) units, operated lunch counters and day rooms. The Warminster NAAFI was hardly the equivalent of the great PX canteens back home. The U.S. agreement with the British required that these canteens serve us everywhere but in London. We fussed about the stale jukebox tunes and always about the food—sausages made of animal fat mixed with farina, greasy eggs, and horrid kidney and pork pies that were often rancid and moldy. We despised tea and declared the national tea-break the primary reason for Britain's failures in the war. We also hated their "sandwiches," small triangles cut from saw-dust bread, smeared with too much butter, on top of which they plunked a shaving of peculiar cucumbers resembling no cucumber of any kind we knew at home. There was never any meat;

fresh mutton, pork, chicken, and beef went to their troops. For dessert, always and forever, stewed green plums, the one fruit British trees produced in abundance.

Yet, there was no apparent shortage of fish-and-chips. We would line up far in advance of a shop's evening opening. Here, we were resented. American money was one thing; our usurpation of this meager national pleasure was another. A large fillet of halibut, plaice, or haddock cooked in a rich flour batter deep-fried, served with browned potato slabs and soaked with vinegar and salt in a cone of newspaper, was as sacred to the Briton as a cozy fireplace and a cup of tea. The local paper featured stories of dying children and old folks whose final wish was for a single orange.

While I personally knew no GIs with English mistresses, many stories circulated of soldiers who swapped U.S. rations for sex.

The visit to Bath goes smoothly. From the outset Stephan says we will go our own way, for he has a date. As the army bus winds through the Wiltshire hills, the war seems remote. Sheep graze on lush pastures marked off by centuries-old hedge rows. Great oaks, elms, and chestnuts shelter herds of heavily-uddered cows. Farmhouses, some with thatched roofs, nestle in sweet valleys. Occasionally, a farmer in brown, gutta percha boots, wearing a slicker, and followed by a sheep dog, treads the road.

In Bath, the bus parks near the eighteenth-century Royal Crescent, a wonder of English architecture built by Christopher Wren. Stephan says I am not to worry if he does not show up by six—he'll have found a spot elsewhere to (sigh) drop his "weary head."

The director of the British hostel is a well-dressed, slender woman of about forty, of the sort you would find entering the vestibule of a country home carrying roses. In plum-like tones, she apologizes for the deprivations of the war, but hopes I will be comfortable during my weekend. She informs me that the bishop of Bath and Wells "on the morrow," is inviting a small group of American soldiers to tea. After Sunday mass she will direct me to transportation. She asks a few perfunctory questions about my family and my plans after the war. Her husband and two sons, all officers, are serving in Asia. They normally live in Belgravia, a fancy suburb of London, but lost their home during the Blitz. She shows me where to sleep and where to stow my overnight bag, then points me towards the Roman baths. There, awed, I fancy old Roman roues seated in and near the waters, stepping always from the same spot down into the pool, eroding stones to foot-shapes. While I can't name the Roman general responsible for the baths, I remember clearly the shapes worn into the stone by the pressings of ancient feet.

At an eighteenth-century pump room where the rich and gouty once drank sulphurous waters hoping for health, I drink from a central marble fountain adorned with cherubs. The water is truly foul. I visit Sally Lunn's Bakery, the oldest house (or so I recall) in Bath, and explore the basement with a guide who points out a small pile of Roman pottery shards. I purloin a scrap which I bring back to Wisconsin, counting it among my favorite possessions.

After touring the cathedral, I sit in the sunny square eating fish-and-chips. Tired of waiting for Stephan, I visit a large antiquarian book shop and spend an hour examining titles, ignorant of what is good and what is not. If a leather cover is stamped in gold I am sure it's valuable. A seventeenth-century book on bee-keeping. A fancy edition of *Paradise Lost*. One of Dickens's novels, published initially in gatherings, is here assembled between single leather covers. The proprietor says that if I find things of interest he will send them to America "cheap." I buy nothing.

Back at the hostel a naked GI in the bunk above mine, at face level, sleeps with his back to me. I sit down fearing to wake him. He turns over, still seemingly asleep with one leg dangling over the bed. I bring my face to his groin.

"Kiss it," he says suddenly.

I redden. "I'm sorry . . . I didn't mean to . . ."

"Take it. It's yours." He draws my hand to his erect penis.

"That's not what I meant." I pull away.

He begins dressing. "You had your chance, bud. I thought we'd have some fun."

I hurry from the room. Later, when I return, he's gone.

Next morning I attend mass, pray for my family before a small altar filled with lighted candles in cranberry-colored sconces, and join a minibus of GIs to see the bishop. Eventually, we reach a villa of pinkish stone, the See. Inside a large vestibule, a sort of atrium, a small cherub fountain spouts water into a pool of lilies. Beyond a pair of French doors is a formal garden where the bishop greets us.

He is a tall muscular man, fiftyish, ruddy, and dressed in full black gaiters, a cleric's white collar, and a black frock coat. He seems to have stepped from an old novel, and has enormous calves which he displays by thrusting his toe forward, flexing the muscles. His walk has a pronounced feminine tilt. His voice is even more plum-like than that of the lady at the hostel who is here assisting the bishop's wife, a portly soul swathed in much velvet and lace. A few women in flimsy floral dresses, inhabitants of adjoining alms houses set up, so we are told, to house the widows and unmarried aging daughters of vicars, proffer a lunch of cucumber sandwiches, tea, and plum tarts served outdoors at a long table covered with butcher paper. Five of us sit on His Eminence's right, and five on his left. He extols the ancient fabric of the cathedral, pretends an enormous interest in our origins, mispronouncing Michigan (calling it Mitch-i-gan), and sets his lips in a perpetual, noncommittal smile. His mind wanders whenever his hand rises absently to a heavy gold chain adorning his chest. After tea, he strides with us about the garden, pointing out roses, telling us their names, and coming finally to a small stream which he claims is filled with trout for his exclusive angling. Before leaving, I manage to get his autograph on a napkin—his name is "Fisher."

Meeting His Eminence does little to broaden my religious views, which were so impaired by the Ft. Jackson chaplain. My glimpse of this self-important bishop is neither warm nor welcoming. My earlier severe Lutheranism has thawed, for I now receive communion from a liberal Methodist attached to our unit. Reverend Froelich's views are Latitudinarian. He does not believe, as Reverend Beckler had, that simply by being born you have violated all ten commandments. He does not maintain that we are hopelessly drenched in sin. Moreover, by failing to secure Beckler's express written approval before taking communion from other than a Missouri Synod Lutheran pastor, I do not "drink damnation unto myself." Eventually, I assist Reverend Froelich at services, ushering and passing out hymnals.

The war in the Pacific, after devastating losses to the Japanese, at last turns in our favor. Rumors are rife that an Allied landing on the Continent, probably in France, is immanent. The number of troops moving through Warminster, processed by our office, doubles. We work twelve-hour days to keep abreast of paper work. My position at headquarters continues to be shaky; a reassignment to an infantry unit in time for D-day is always possible.

Our immediate source for news, apart from the BBC broadcasts received over the few personal radios on base, is the daily *Stars and Stripes*. The publishers boast that it is a foot soldier's paper, not designed either to glamorize the war or to please the brass. After reading the latest front-page update of battlefront events, we turn avidly to dog faces Joe and Willie—the doughboys in Bill Mauldin's famous cartoons.

For my nineteenth birthday, on October 20, 1944, I first visit London, on a leave planned by Sandy Troxell, a tall Californian, a corporal, with shocks of black hair, who had grown up on a ranch and speaks with cowboy twang. He is a friend of Stephan's. He boasts of having sex with a ranch lass who liked doing it in the barn against the side of a recumbent, cud-chewing cow. How naive does he think I am? I know he's fibbing.

We arrive in London at 9:00 on a foggy night, the troop bus unloading on the south bank of the Thames, opposite Victoria Station. With the city in full blackout, stagnant with fog, you sense the surreal excitement of teeming, semi-visible people. We cross a long bridge, the only lights the gleaming ends of cigarettes and an occasional flash from the Thames far below, the only sounds the subdued *put put* of barges and cargo boats.

In the packed streets, a few lorries, ambulances, and taxis with dimmed amber sidelights roll past. There is coal soot and diesel fumes, and coughing, jostling bodies. Troxell, who has earlier visited London, declares it a pickpocket's dream, advising that I secure my wallet. Linking arms so as not to lose one another, we head for Leicester Square, to an American USO hostel where we hire beds, English cots with straw mattresses and woolen blankets.

We eat meals at a U. S. military diner situated in a posh hotel. The food is basic—plenty of steak, pork chops, mashed potatoes, and tons of ice cream, cherry cobbler, and apple pie.

Picadilly Circus is so jammed with pedestrians that vehicle traffic is detoured. Whores, mostly in pairs, perambulate through gaggles of waiting men. One creature asks for a cigarette. I oblige, lighting up her face. She is hardly more than a girl, her lips smeared red. She gropes me, offering to suck me for five shillings. "I'll be quick," she says. I pull away to find Troxell leaning against the Eros Fountain being fellated. The woman keeps her hat on, one with cloth cherries, resembling those black-brimmed affairs worn by Rita Hayworth and Loretta Young. Troxell pumps the whore's mouth, making short explosive whimpers until he shudders and comes. "Let's go," I say to Troxell.

"Why? The evening's young." He waits near a semi-circular wall behind the fountain, the palms of his hands turned back against the stone. He drops his pants again. In the glow of a match I see his hard-on. Two more women go down on him.

"I needed that," he says. "No hassle, no beds, no VD. Just a slam-bam, thank you, ma'am."

On the way back to the hostel an air-raid siren wails. Aged wardens, wearing arm bands, herd us into an underground shelter, the Picadilly Circus tube stop. The station is crowded. After the all-clear (less than an hour passes), we return to the streets which are already crammed with people.

The next day, my birthday, we tour the Tower of London. Impressive are Henry VIII's armor and the cell in which Sir Walter Raleigh was imprisoned. We wander up Fleet Street to St. Paul's, closed because of blitz damage. Most of the adjacent area is in ruin, and though the rubble has been cleared no rebuilding has begun.

After a hefty steak dinner, complete with a small birthday cake (arranged for by Troxell), we take in a mediocre J. Arthur Rank film set in gas-light London, a Jack the Ripper saga, and then return to the Eros Fountain.

"You saw that one, didn't you?" Troxell asks. "That was a man dressed like a woman."

In the shadows the figure appears as a hatless female of medium height.

"How do you know?" I ask.

"For starters, no woman sucks cock as good as a man. When she took my money, I saw her hairy arm."

The next night, with Troxell on a date by himself, I attend a USO dance. The high point is the appearance of Sir Harry Lauder, then in his eighties, dressed in kilts, wielding his famous polished crooked walking stick. In his time Lauder was a singer and comedian incredibly popular on both sides of the Atlantic. In Wisconsin, the small stack of 78 records which I played on a wind-up Victrola included his classic "Oh, How I Hate To Get Up On Sunday Morning" and "Wee Bonnie Lassie."

The massed ballroom quiets. Sir Harry delivers warm remarks to us Americans before he launches into a set of his vintage songs. I hope for his autograph, but he's whisked away.

As for the dance itself, the USO imports a bevy of English school girls from Henley-on-Thames as a contribution to the war effort. An orchestra burbles genteel waltzes and fox trots heavy in the strings. Jitterbugging is discouraged. I find myself loving my partner's soft hair and skin. Her name is Elissa.

"Another dance?" I ask, leading her to a table for lemonade.

"I'm sorry," she says. "We can dance only one set with a soldier. The headmistress would be displeased."

"How can I get to know you?" I ask, clearing my throat. Elissa is a brunette with hair styled in waves evocative of the 1920s and has a clear white complexion with hints of rose. I'm in love.

"I'm sorry," she says, giving me an unexpected kiss on the cheek. "That's against the rules, too."

The girls disappear to a waiting bus, and while some men linger, others set out to wander the streets.

Off Leicester Square I find a theater featuring the "final show" of one of Europe's most famous legends, the burlesque queen Phyllis Dixie. *Phyllis Dixie in "Peek-a-Boo Again."* Though ancient, she appears luscious with the help of feathers, distance, and soft lighting. The American audience hoots, yells, and screams for her to "take it off." Hawkers sell candy kisses, each box containing a celluloid kewpie doll in bra and panties. Dixie belts several songs, delivers double-entendres, and prances about to the screeching orchestra. In less than an hour the show concludes with inflated cupids flying out of calyxes and the goddess herself swishing fans and disappearing without encores.

The days sweep by, the most memorable event being the shedding of our regular uniforms for Eisenhower jackets and combat boots. The entire army switches, probably out of pride in the new commander of the European theater of operations. The trim Eisenhower jacket with its broad chest and its narrow waist greatly enhances the GI image. And the hightop boots, worn hitherto only by marines and the paratroops, now are ours. The uniforms are grace notes for the awesome event soon to transpire, on June 6, 1944, D-day.

On the 8th of November our unit leaves Warminster for France.

4

France: November 1944

ON A CLOUDY November night we hoisted anchor in Southampton Harbor, headed for the English Channel, and six
miles out transferred to a fleet of landing craft. The Channel
was calm, a bonus since we debarked down a rope lattice, with full
gear, to the waiting LSTs. Floodlights blazed. The officers supervised
our descent. Our big-buttocked CO gazed timorously round when his
turn came and his plump hands clutched rungs as his polished boots
sought purchase. We cheered when he lowered himself into our midst.
On the LST, the ideal place was the leeward side away from the cold
where I huddled with Troxell.

Dawn revealed a gray morning, low chalky cliffs, and a large dour
town. A scattering of Allied vessels anchored in the harbor.

We debarked south of the cliffs, the LSTs cutting their motors a hundred yards out. Dropped doors formed a walkway over which we proceeded in a ragged file. Drizzle had set in. We were south of Omaha
Beach, which explained the dearth of wrecked ships, tanks, and trucks.
We hiked most of that day, following a gravel road inland through
dunes, and reached an almost treeless expanse of hilly terrain. There
were ruined half-timbered farmhouses, but no signs of life, either human or animal. Shortly, because of the humidity, we were soaked. The
straps of my pack cut so that I walked with my thumbs under the straps.

At Le Havre we threaded our hushed way through nightmarish
devastation. Not a single dwelling was intact. Some houses, as many as
four stories high, had their sides sheared, exposing walls adorned with
family pictures and plumbing suspended over floorless space. A
stench of leaking gas, charred wood, and sickly geraniums suffused
everything with a noisome odor. Bodies still lay beneath the rubble; it
would take weeks to retrieve them.

In a cold afternoon rain, in a field adjacent to a pine and chestnut forest, we erected pup tents in haphazard lines, two men per tent. A floor of thick grass beaten flat by the rain made for comfort but our canvas, though "water-treated," leaked when touched.

The cooks, with their stoves and gear sheltered under sweeps of canvas, served hot foot. Clouds of steam rose from aluminum trays of chicken fricassee, mashed potatoes, and pie.

Before chow I was detailed to dig slit trenches for latrines. Finished, muddy mess kits in hand, we were served. Eating inside a cramped tent was impracticable, so we ate in the rain, bolting our food before it was unpalatably drenched. Our former Warminster barracks seemed like the Ritz Carleton. There were huge blisters on the balls of my feet which I pierced with a knife, cutting the shredded flesh, waiting for the watery burn to ease.

Near day-break, a brisk wind heralded an ever-brightening sun, enhancing our spirits. Our clothes, however, remained rain-soaked, making our packs twice as heavy as usual. The day's hike, a sergeant informed us, would surpass yesterday's. Breakfast included powdered eggs, the last of the British bread we so despised (the mess sergeant promised we'd have "American" bread soon), fried Spam, and potatoes and onions drowned in bacon grease. Since I had helped excavate the latrine, perverse Army logic required that I help fill it in.

Rural Normandy, rife with a crazy patchwork of ancient hedge rows, resembled rural England. But a closer look revealed differences. France was more expansive, and the pastures, orchards, and fields much larger. A permeating violet glow grew more pronounced as we proceeded inland. Trees laden with apples, plums, and pears flourished within hand's reach. We filled our helmets with fruit.

After a two-day march, we reached an army camp recently evacuated by the French. While we respected the British soldier, we didn't respect the *poilu*. Hadn't they abandoned their vaunted Maginot Line? Their camps seemed evidence of inept discipline and foul hygiene. "The Tired and Sick French!" we exclaimed.

This camp, once permanent, thoroughly justified our prejudices. Americans never quit a site without policing it. Even in snow and rain we were put through the "asses and elbows" routine, shouted at and cursed by NCOs, until we had gleaned every scrap of debris, including cigarette butts, throwing them into a common sump.

In uniform, France, 1945.

The French camp was itself a sump, the streets littered with maggot-ridden food scraps, bones, old mattresses, and wine bottles (many of them smashed). In the barracks, mattresses stained with urine sagged on wire cots. The footlockers were crushed and haspless. The latrines, foul with piles of excrement, buzzed with enormous flies.

Even at their best, French latrines were regressively primitive; for, what you found was not a porcelain commode and seat, but a porcelain or tiled floor with raised foot rests to accommodate your shoes, with a hole in the floor into which your anus, if you were lucky, exuded its droppings. You hunkered like cave men evacuating in the only posture guaranteed not to soil your hairy heels. When the plumbing worked, waters round your feet sloshed away the excrement. A few unlucky souls, using old brooms and shovels abandoned by the French, were detailed to clean the mess. The commanding officer ordered slit-trenches, a series of which, surrounded by green canvas wind breakers, soon appeared near the camp.

After a week's bivouac, we proceeded to a junction of roads called Mailly le Camp, ten miles southwest of Troyes, Aube, where we stayed for six months. Troxell, I discovered later, joined an infantry unit in Germany. I was assigned to headquarters as a clerk-typist. For the first time, I saw German prisoners of war, work details presided over by Sgt. Mike Sarkowsky, a regular army man who bullied and beat them.

My reaction to the Germans was a mix of attraction and fear. They were easy to berate. Their faded and tattered uniforms were derelict, and their few insignias of unit and rank, still polished and bright, were a pathetic contrast. Most wore visored Luftwaffe caps and tunics. Some were mere boys, hardly past adolescence; the oldest were in their forties. Most had boils and catarrhs. Their wretched food, a bare life-sustaining diet, simulated what men in prisons received—bread and potatoes and slivers of beef and pork wafted through a thin gruel of noodles or rice. To qualify for sick-call (fortunately, one prisoner was a physician) they ran the gauntlet of Kowalcyzk's beatings.

As clerical assistant to Ed Oaks, the first sergeant, I shortly received my first promotion, to private first class. Within hours I had sewn stripes on all my clothes. The "T" below the chevron signified that my skills were in technical or clerical areas. In Troyes I posed for pictures to send home, the stripe proudly displayed. In one shot my hair stands up as a wild mass—I was letting it grow from the Marine cut I had worn in England. My sideburns are ineptly clipped, tonsured, so it appears,

49

with kitchen shears. My eyes sit deep in their hollows, shadowed as eyes in mug shots are often shadowed. One full-length portrait is better. Standing on a cheap Turkish rug, posed against a fake studio window with a gauzy, floor-to-ceiling curtain, hands on hips, wearing my winter ODs, I manage a smile. My mother said I looked older, more "fleshed out."

Sergeant Oaks was a stocky, blonde Missourian in his mid-thirties with a swayed back. His failing was cognac. I frequently covered for him. I would receive reveille reports, check the field phones, and execute any papers the new CO, Lieutenant Farmer, required. Eventually, Oaks would show up abashed and smiling, a cigarette dangling from his lips, ask if anyone had missed him, and start ruffling through papers on his desk.

I filed documents, directives, orders and memos in elaborate systems. I developed a peculiar shorthand, a mix of Palmer method strokes and partially-formed key words. I loved locating documents, no matter how arcane, promptly. I often spent evenings at my desk.

Lieutenant Farmer, a Virginian, swarthy with a fleshy nose and brown eyes, lamented being "glued" to his desk. On D-day, shrapnel had damaged his legs. I typed his weekly memos to headquarters asking for a transfer back to the field. "There's a glut of officers now," he complained. One of his charges was Sarkowsky and the POW detail.

Sarkowsky's strut made him seem a parody of Erich von Stroheim in World War I films. His stripes were so bright we imagined he'd painted them on with silver paint. Garbed in fatigues, his stripes most visible, wearing a webbed belt and sidearms, he paraded his Germans, shouting orders frosted with obscenities. Lieutenant Farmer, observing Sarkowsky, would chew him out, insisting that a true soldier knows compassion, even for prisoners. Sarkowsky would salute, turn, and leave the office, sneering at "civilians."

I wait inside a tent with rifle ready, live ammunition in the breech, with orders from Sarkowsky to shoot any prisoner even thinking of escape. Where would they hide if they ran off? The French are hostile.

The prisoners huddle in small shivering groups. A blonde youth hangs off by himself. He hasn't shaved for days, something certain to exorcise Sarkowsky. He approaches me. A yard away, his arms rigidly at his sides, he asks in perfect English: "Can you help? I am ill." He looks feverish. "My throat is sore." He touches the spot. "I can't swallow."

"Wait for the sergeant," I say, bringing my rifle up. Sarkowsky arrives. "He needs a doctor," I say, pointing to the youth.

"He's fuckin' off," declares Sarkowsky.

"Look at him," I insist. "He's not lying. He's on fire."

"Ok, Peters," Sarkowsky says. "March him to the medics. But be alert! You can't trust Krauts, even sick ones."

Later that week the soldier dies.

Sarkowsky in a cold rain, clad in a rubber slicker and rain hat, beats a German kneeling in mud. The German clutches a heel of bread. As Sarkowsky pummels him, knocking off his soaked Luftwaffe cap, the man closes his fist over the soggy bread which pulps and runs through his fingers. Like an obsessed rooster, Sarkowsky hops around the sad figure whipping his head, back, shoulders, and face. The German streams blood. None of us protests. Then Lieutenant Farmer appears and orders Sarkowsky to cease. When Sarkowsky raises his arm to strike new blows, Farmer grabs Sarkowsky's whip and, on the spot, demotes him to private and orders him to a unit processing GIs for service in Germany.

A popular Tent City diversion was gambling. Troyes, the largest nearby town, was ten miles away; you needed a lift from the motor pool to get there. Monthly liquor rations were generous. The officers' supply was free. Enlisted men drew lots for the best booze. Drinking occurred both in a day room and in our tents. For privacy, we preferred the latter. I managed cognac highs two or three times a week, pouring the liquor into my aluminum mess kit cup and drinking it straight. An acrid metallic taste sensitized your teeth.

My favorite drinking buddies were Mike Mulrooney, a corporal from Minneapolis; Bert Siever from Pierre, South Dakota, who as a result of a wound had a bone depression above his right eye; and George Perkins from Bangor, Maine, a chunky, dark-haired man with a brainy humor rendered in an inimitable Maine accent. He succeeded Sarkowsky as the NCO in charge of prisoners. He designed a soccer field for the Germans and joined the games. At the University of Maine, where he studied law, he played on the varsity team. He urged me to get an education. During much of that summer we lay on blankets in the burnt grass reading and talking, working up tans. He browned easily while I burned and peeled.

Siever was more homespun that Perkins, six years older, married,

A studio shot taken in Troyes, France, 1945.

In camp just outside Troyes, 1945.

and by trade a linotype operator. I accompanied him on numerous walks over fields and through copses. One walk took an entire afternoon, our destination a thatched country inn called *Ma Chaumière* (My Thatched Cottage) run by a plump French woman, Madame Dovier, and a teen-aged daughter. The inn had whitewashed stone walls with windows and trellises filled with climbing roses. The squat building was once thatched, the modern roof maintaining the scalloped pattern over the doors and around the windows and eaves. A pair of white metal tables and chairs sat in a rear garden crammed with roses, geraniums, and hollyhocks. Here we had coffee, wine, slabs of bread, and eggs fried in butter. The daughter, barely pubescent, would linger, thrusting her small stomach forward, emphasizing her tiny breasts. Her sallow blonde hair was always freshly curled, the ringlets fashioned by rolling her hair in paper, the result resembling a tangle of sweet pea vines. The mother gave the girl pats, encouraging her to be forward.

A lanky, black-haired GI in his mid-thirties slunk in the background. He wore and OD shirt, trousers, and combat boots, but with no insignia. I never heard his name. Between our minimal French and the fractured English Mme. Dovier spoke, we understood that the Yank was her lover. She boasted that when he married her she would sell *Ma Chaumière* and live in Alabama, where he owned a radio shop. On our third visit, the man joined us, sipping wine at our patio table. When a jeep approached (the inn was on the main road to Troyes) he jumped up and disappeared. He later told us that he had served with Patton's tank corps, had separated from his unit in crossing the Oise, and suffered amnesia, sleeping in woods and barns, until arriving finally at Mme. Dovier's. He intended to rejoin his unit, he said. When Siever offered to take him back to our camp, he smiled, put his arm around Mme. Dovier, and said he would stay where he was—his amnesia was improving.

"We all fight in our own way," said Siever.

"You mean we won't turn him in?"

"Let's wait and see," Siever said. Two weeks later the man was gone. Mme. Dovier tearfully reported that the military police arrested him. "I never see him after that," she said. "He was good to me."

One sultry afternoon, as Siever and I traversed a grove of oaks bordering a river, we heard voices: "Yank. Yank." Two women moored a dumpy boat and ran toward us. Both wore short summery gingham dresses and embroidered bolero jackets. Both were hatless. One was raven-haired, the other brunette. They were giggling. The brunette started to draw Siever towards the boat. *"Venez! Venez!"* she urged. The other girl, less forward, lingered, waiting for me. Her black eyebrows met over the bridge of a substantial white nose. A wash of hair adorned her upper lip, and she had very white teeth. ·

"Michelle," she said, taking my hand.

"Bob," I said, which she repeated as "Bop."

"Let's go." Siever moved towards the boat. "We're invited."

I offered to row, and doffed my shirt, shoes, and socks. The sun felt delicious. Siever and the brunette, René, in the stern, embraced, kissing. Michelle in the prow secured a picnic basket. After twenty minutes we reached a sheltered beach dotted with crude, unpainted mooring posts.

Siever and René dashed up the bank. Once they disappeared, Michelle dropped her skirt. *"Nageons!"* she exclaimed, inviting me after her into the river. *"Venez. Venez."* Her legs and underarms were hairy, a triangle of pubic hair reached almost to her naval, and her large breasts were freckled. When I delayed, she emerged, dripping, and unbuckled my trousers. *"Venez!"* she shouted, grabbing my hand. I plunged in and swam some thirty yards from shore. Reaching me she thrust her legs around mine and began sucking my lip, probing with her tongue. She tried to insert my penis. My shorts, a ridiculous brown mass, floated off downstream. Then she struck out for the opposite bank. I turned, reached the boat, and secured my trousers.

"Je suis jolie, non?" Michelle asked, pouting. I gave a non-committal smile.

We found Siever and René beneath a huge tree. Siever's buttocks glistened as he pumped in the missionary position. Michelle started laughing. "I'll be goddamned." Siever shuddered, rolling over.

"We'll be by the boat," I said.

The girls spread a gingham cloth and, from their hamper, produced bread, white cheese, and red wine. After we ate we offered the girls cigarettes. Siever arranged to meet René the next day. She asked him to bring some toilet soap.

On our way back to camp, I nagged Siever. "You're married," I said. "I don't understand . . . "

"It don't matter," he said. "She wants soap and cigarettes. I want a fuck."

"There's VD."

"Short arm inspection." He struck my shoulder. "Don't be a prude, Peters. You might be dead before you know it."

"But I'm a virgin."

"That's why we went up the hill. You could fuck Michelle. You'll rot if you go back home with your cherry. Even Mary had a baby!"

The next day, alone, I followed the river south, coming to a cove where an old willow thrust a huge lyre-shaped branch over the water, a branch smoothed by diving feet. I stripped, sunning myself, then fell asleep, to be awakened by three French boys. I grabbed my clothes, but before I could dress, they asked for cigarettes. They stripped and sat nearby smoking and chattering. They were just under conscription age, with the sturdy, black-haired pulchritude of French farm boys. They hunkered as they smoked, their uncut penises snaking between their legs. Then they began to rough-house, displaying themselves in various postures before leaping into the stream, diving from the willow. They gestured for me to follow, which I did. For over an hour we gamboled and dove. Their abandon was contagious. Later, as they relaxed in the sun, their heads on one another's breasts, I envied their intimacies.

"You like *les femmes*?" one of them asked. "*Zig-zag*," said another, inserting his penis through a circle formed by his thumb and forefinger. His friends laughed. "We like *beaucoup de zig-zag*," one declared. Then suddenly they wrestled the masturbator in a whirl of manic energy which quickly spent itself. Soon they dressed and strode off into the forest. For days afterwards, I fantasized about making love to them, individually and together, even waking at night, sweating, unable to shake their images. I returned to the river several times, but they never reappeared.

The farm buildings of our laundress were of heavy whitewashed timbers positioned around a quadrangle and a large metal pump. Gigantic piles of manure and straw covered most of the north side of a cattle barn. Chickens wandered freely, pecking pebbles and seeds. The house, whitewashed, faced a gravel road with a large garden of asters, roses, bachelor buttons, geraniums, and daisies. Fields and orchards of apple, pear, and peach trees shone through gaps between the buildings. The woman had lost two sons fighting on the German front. Her husband was a prisoner near Dresden.

She heated water, all pumped by hand, in large wooden tubs over outdoor fires. She bleached our clothes in a mix of boiling water, lye, and ashes. We furnished the soap. She put the wash through two rinses. Later, she ironed and creased our shirts with dampened paper. Her irons resembled the flatirons my mother used, heating them also on a wood stove, a tedious chore. The woman often wept, missing her husband and sons. We paid her with Camel cigarettes, which she bartered for black market meat and cloth. Occasionally, she served wine. Her kitchen held geraniums and pictures of relatives, the men stern and weather-beaten, the women resembling those painted by Van Gogh. A damp of rancid sweat and sweet violets, the attar of generations, pervaded the fieldstone walls. In both living room and kitchen were faded rotogravures of Jesus with exposed bleeding heart.

During most twilight hours, civilians carrying gunny bags gathered opposite the camp fence. We appeared with our pockets stuffed with food from the mess hall and with personal rations of cigarettes, candy, and gum. Such activities were illegal, and could result in severe penalties, especially if you sold blankets, sheets, or army clothing. The French brought eggs, wine, and francs (which we spent in Troyes). Occasionally they produced clocks, cameras, and binoculars.

A new friend, Mike Hart, married, was a mechanic in a Pennsylvania coal mine. He reminded me of my dad, craggy, Aryan, broad shouldered, with small hips. His thin mouth also resembled Dad's. One day he vowed to get me laid. "You keep talking tits and pussy," he laughed. "So put up or shut up."

"Yes," I said, "Take me to Paris."

My boasting was smoke; it was really Hart I wanted.

In Paris we were assaulted by odors I have ever since associated with that city—Galouise cigarettes, cognac, perfume, horse sweat, and automobile exhaust. Mike booked a hotel near the Gare de l'Est rather than take USO billets. "We'll be more apt to find women," he said.

Our funky room had two beds, one double, one twin. A strange object resembling a toilet bowl without a top, Mike explained, was a bidet. "It's for washing French pussy."

We wandered Montmartre and the Rue Pigalle. Street musicians, sword swallowers, and snake charmers crammed the chestnut, tree-lined esplanade. Skimpily dressed women, some in outrageous makeup, hung about in lavish display near bistros. One henna-haired creature walked up to me. "*Zig-Zag*?" She stated her price in broken

English, and said she had a room across the street. "Two for one," she said after Mike waved her off. "Poufs!" she jeered, giving the sign of the fig.

I visited the Louvre while Mike opted for a new Betty Grable film near the Concorde. As naive as I was about art, I had at least heard of the Venus di Milo. Her pose suggested she had dropped something she was about to stoop to retrieve. I walked round and round, enchanted. I pressed my palm against the small of her back, where the soft roll of buttock begins, and felt her warm flesh.

In adjacent galleries, male nudes, so nonchalant in their nakedness beneath sculpted muscle, were balanced in quiescent, almost female postures. Their phalluses surprised me. Were Phidias and the other artists so anxious for a total harmony that they eschewed large penises? Or were they themselves short, and doing their bit for all Greeks less well-endowed by fashioning them into images of eternal art? I edged closer to another GI who seemed as absorbed as I. He looked over, widened his eyes, and smiled: "Enjoying it?" I choked out an embarrassed "yes" and moved off.

That evening we explored the Champs-Élysées, passing the Church of the Madeleine, the stop where military buses arrived and departed. The famous church with its tawny Greek columns resembled banks I had seen in London. The facade, rational for a true church, reeked of stability, property, and wealth.

At twilight, lurid females with leather purses solicited business, gathering at military buses even before the doors opened to spew GIs forth. Despite their anxiety to turn tricks, the women, observing a decorum with one another, avoided pushing and shoving. Most claimed hotel rooms nearby. In the fading light their faces glared with makeup. I hung back, observing, imagining teeth smeared with bloody lipstick.

At the Place de la Concorde we read notices of the guillotines, and continued up the esplanade, beneath the famous chestnuts, towards the Arc-de-Triomphe. Even under wartime restrictions, Paris was *the* city of light. Walkers were everywhere. Jets of decorative water sprayed forth, glimmering with color. Sidewalk cafes (and they were expensive) were jammed, spilling onto the streets, forcing pedestrians to move dangerously close to autos streaming past towards the great round-about encircling the Arc. The latter was resplendent. Its images of soldiers with weapons, flags, and ordonnance seemed sculpted from rich cake.

The concierge, a fat lady with masses of unkempt emerald hair, wearing an over-sized, gray sweater, seated behind a mesh screen, with a hairless poodle in her lap, looks up suspiciously before thrusting our key at us. The dog rolls back its egg-white eyes and gives a weak yip. At a urinal tray in the narrow main corridor, as we are relieving ourselves, two women appear. Mike has engaged them for the evening.

Our third-floor room reeks of sex, generations of bad smoke, and damp fraying wallpaper adorned with faded fleur de lys. A dim, red-shaded lamp sits on a stand near a sagging double bed. There's also a single cot. By sitting on one bed you can easily touch the other. A pale blue dressing table has a tri-partite scalloped mirror, navel high, positioned to reflect the beds. A grimy pair of French windows give onto the street.

The women are chunky blondes in frayed tailored suits with tight, brief skirts, who appear to be sisters. They wear cloche hats. Mike negotiates a price, which the women request in advance. "Is that OK?" Mike asks me. "You're willing?" The whores wait side by side near the door, ready to depart if the terms are wrong.

"Sure," I say, vowing not to spoil the evening. The younger whore, whose Clara Bow lips are bright orange, sits waiting on Mike's bed. "She *zig-zag* with you," she says, pointing to her sister. She strikes a match and lights a cigarette. In the glow her ivory face bones are positioned behind wells of nasal cartilage.

"It's my treat, Peters. Relax. Enjoy."

The room chokes with sexual dust.

"I'm sorry, Mike, I'm sorry." I feel like a jerk. The usual smear of rationalizations: maintaining my virginity for a future wife, violating biblical interdictions, fear of venereal disease, but above all the fear that I will fail and be ridiculed. I am far too naive to let my body guide me; bullets could never, it seemed, drop effortlessly from my gun chamber. In my fantasy, sex with males would be easy; I knew their bodies as I knew mine. Narcissus pressing his glowing lips against his own lips in a pool. I swept my hand through ashes in a sterile grate.

Impatient, my whore leaves the hotel. I tell Mike I'll go off by myself, so as not to interfere with his pleasure.

"No," he says. "Have a stab later if you want." He laughs.

If I had roses I would give them to him.

His whore undresses and crawls between the sheets. Mike strips.

From my bed, I can almost touch his back. His hairy wrist caresses the woman's face. Her mouth is ajar, baring her teeth. Her eyes close their cerise-colored lids. She arches her back as Mike mounts her. Bands of street light fall in swathes across Mike's buttocks. Shortly, ejaculatory sounds waft through the room.

The room quiets. A neon sign flashes through the drapes. Carousing voices in the street. Cats pitch hot screams followed by moans.

"Bob, are you awake?"

"Yes." I sit up.

"Come on over. Have a feel before she leaves. She won't care. There's a condom on the table."

I feel silly standing in my shapeless GI shorts.

"*Oui, oui,*" says the whore, drawing me to the bed. She unbuttons my shorts. As I slide between the sheets, she begins fondling my penis. I kiss her breasts, which seem puckered as though she recently nursed a child. She fits the condom, then clasps me, throwing her legs around my thighs. I slide between her legs. I thrust past a ridge of bone and into a moist hollow. I caress the lips of her vagina, inserting my fingers along my cock spine. As I approach orgasm, I strike a wart! "You trew? You trew?"

Simulating an orgasm, I climb off and at the bidet flush the rubber before she knows I have not come. The ruse works. She washes me, sits on the bed, smokes a cigarette, then dresses and departs.

"How was it?" Mike asks.

"OK," I reply. "But no violins or choirs in the sky."

"Well, let's get some sleep."

Mike sleeps with an arm thrown over my chest.

At noon we visit a VD station, one of several scattered through Paris where, if you shoot antiseptic jell up your glans, within twenty-four hours of having sex, you'll escape the clap. In the privacy of a cubicle, I treat myself. After a hefty breakfast at a U. S. Army commissary restaurant, we catch the train to Troyes.

By December 1944, the Allied armies approached the German frontier. Spearheading the action was the U.S. 7th Army, which included the 106th Infantry, my unit at Fort Jackson. Major drives were launched near Aachen and in the Saar. Of necessity, Allied troops were thin in other areas, and Supreme Headquarters, Allied Expeditionary Force assumed that the Germans would hesitate to launch counter attacks, given the rough mountain terrain between Monshau and the Moselle.

On December 16, in extraordinarily heavy fog, the Germans attacked near Bastogne, in the Battle of the Bulge. My former regiment, the 422nd, was pivotal. Despite massive deployments directed by Eisenhower, assisted by Generals Montgomery, Patton, and Bradley, the Germans made deep penetrations towards the Meuse, their immediate target. Not until January 15, 1945, did the Allies restore their positions. Although the Germans failed, they delayed Allied. operations for six weeks. The Germans lost 250,000 men, the Allies 60,000.

On April 12, 1945, we are ordered into formation. "At ease!" shouts the Battalion Commander. "This morning, the president died. Harry Truman is now president."

The shock registers slowly. How gray the sand looks, and streaks of reddish blackberry shrubs tangle themselves in gray meshed wire. Two outraged swallows pursue a hawk. A vigorous wind ruffles my shirt.

"Dismissed!"

We linger stunned. With such news do you move in circles? Do you sit? Do you touch someone? Do you lament in private?

We all knew of Roosevelt's polio, and we had seen the recent photos of him wearing a huge woolen cape against the cold, at Yalta, with Churchill and Stalin. Yet, despite his ill-health and aging, we assumed he would survive the war. His domestic programs during the thirties kept us from starving. My father had labored building roads for forty dollars a month under the first WPA program; and Roosevelt's food relief programs assured that we would eat. We bought our house and forty acres through the Home Owners' Loan Corporation. Poor, we felt that Roosevelt cared. Many of us saw Truman as a wimp chosen by Roosevelt as running mate because he would never rock boats as Henry Wallace had done.

Slowly, events re-shaped themselves, and our various routines, including boredom, prevailed. The Italian campaign under General Mark Clark and his 15th Army Group was succeeding. The Russians invaded Germany. On April 28, anti-Fascists captured Mussolini as he was escaping with his mistress Carla Petracci and executed them. We saw the pictures of the pair beaten and bloody, strung upside down like hogs. The Germans continued to retreat, their many cities abandoned in ruin. On the other side of the globe, although we had freed the Philippines and Okinawa, Tojo's forces remained frightening adversaries. Win Europe first was the Allied policy.

Eligible for furloughs, I took few. I avoided visiting Rome and Athens, and my trips to Paris were brief and superficial. Perhaps I was too reticent and preferred comfortable routines. In awe of literary figures, I failed to visit Gertrude Stein and Alice B. Toklas at one of their "at homes" held for GIs. She saw Americans as "far too serious," and advised them to "smile at at least one Frenchman a day." Most of my army buddies had never heard of her. At her salon, I probably would have stood oafishly about, stumbled over garden pathway stones, and stammered if she addressed me.

My new furlough was to England. I would travel with Bill Turney, the company clerk who was a close friend. Though usually placid, he could be energetic and humorous. He was slender, auburn-haired, and exuded the maturity I liked in friends. He seemed older than I.

On May 2nd, 1945, we entrained for Dieppe, crossed by ferry to Dover, and reached London by rail where we spent a night before traveling north to Edinburgh, arriving mid-morning on May 5th. At a bread and breakfast place on a quiet side street near the Walter Scott Monument, we stowed our gear and began to explore the city. Newsboys were crying Hitler's disappearance. Berchtesgaden (site of the famous eyrie) and Salzburg had capitulated to the Allies. Munich was about to fall.

Edinburgh was drenched in light. The famous castle on its remote hill glimmered, brightening the dour stones with lemon and lavender. Visitors wandering the keep and ramparts resembled bits of gossamer glued to sticks. Nearby, Scott's monument, with stone filigrees, looked absurdly inept—if the design was to protect the statue from the elements. My reverence for Scott was both ill-informed and intense— intense because his greatness in itself inculcated awe, and mindless because the only work by him I had read was *The Lady of the Lake*, as a freshman in high school. Simply to walk the streets he once traversed was exciting. I naively fantasized that via osmosis his verve and brilliance would nourish me. Moreover, the Scottish author I was named for, Robert Louis Stevenson, also lived in Edinburgh. As a tot I owned his *A Child's Garden of Verses*, one of the three books in my library, the others being *Tom Swift and His Sky Train* and *Robinson Crusoe*. Both of the latter bored me.

Below the monument, a flowered bank ran steeply to a crowded esplanade. Ageratums, marigolds, irises, and petunias formed intricate geometric designs, the centerpiece being an enormous clock face fashioned entirely of variegated flowers. The most impressive buds were of a purple so intense they approached the color of blood.

On the 6th, after a visit to Edinburgh Castle, Turney and I took a bus to the suburbs for horseback riding. At a stables we hired horses and a guide, the latter a skinny man in a soiled tweed suit who spoke with a genteel accent. "I've groomed horses for years," he boasted. "These two, Bess and Rose, are mare and daughter. You'll like them. Good temperaments. They won't throw you."

I had never ridden before. Bill had grown up with horses. His mother was a hurdles champion. As a child I had feared the animal and would never consent either to lead, follow behind, or ride my uncle's horses, powerful drays we hired for plowing our fields.

Bill mounted the lead horse, a chestnut mare. My horse, the younger, followed Bill's, cantering when she cantered, slowing when she slowed. Since I was unable to catch the stride, my hip bones clapped painfully against the saddle. Whenever we galloped I suffered and had to stop. Feeling guilty for reducing Bill's pleasure, I insisted on returning to the stables.

"OK," he said, disappearing through a copse. "It's all in the rhythm, he later said. "Watch Dale Evans. See how she does it."

Prince Street teemed with girls walking in pairs, the whores distinguished by leather purses flopped over their arms. Shop girls and secretaries in cheaper clothes wore their hair in soft rolls round their skulls. Popular were small felt hats resembling overturned meat pies, of the sort worn by Joan Crawford, Greer Garson, and Donna Reed. Newsboys hawked rumors that the Germans (Hitler remained invisible) would capitulate. By early evening the streets were jammed with people anticipating the end of the war in Europe.

"See those two," Bill said.

We approached.

"Cooling your heels?" Bill asked.

The girls, both redheads, exchanged glances. "What do you mean?" asked the taller of the pair. She was full-bosomed and wore a halter top drawn behind her neck.

Bill offered cigarettes. "You look like you're tired of walking."

"True," the girl laughed.

"Edinburgh will go crazy if the war is really over," Bill said, easing down by the taller girl. "Don't mind if we sit, do you? This is my buddy Bob."

Both girls, typists, lived in the northern part of the city. They told us of a pub nearby where Scott, Burns, and Stevenson drank. One girl boasted she'd never read a single work by the trio.

The pub was crowded. Behind the bar were books by the worthies. All copies looked faded and well-thumbed. We found an ingle where we sat drinking Guinness. The girls were coquettish. When I tried to kiss my date she withdrew. "Not here," she said. Bill wasn't getting very far either. "Let's go to the park," he said.

We exited the pub, the girls leading the way, and found a secluded spot where we began necking.

"Something stinks," my date exclaimed, sitting up. There was an acrid, oleaginous smell.

"My god, Bill. I've rolled in dog shit!" The patch on my leg was as big as a dinner plate.

"Well," said Bill, "that takes care of tonight."

On May 7th, 1945, at 2:41 A.M., General Jodl signed the act of surrender, to be effective at midnight on the 8th. The treaty was ratified in Berlin on the 9th.

On the 8th we awoke to pandemonium. Walking the promenade was nearly impossible. People were already shouting, kissing, drinking, and dancing. By early afternoon revellers overwhelmed the city. Assisted by police, workers cordoned off an area where they erected a wooden platform with railings adorned with ribbons, flags, and balloons. Bagpipe bands played patriotic songs, many inspired by Robert Burns. Never had I been in such a crush. Hands flew through the air, grabbing us, rejoicing that the nightmare was over.

Just after dark, Sir Harry Lauder, an aged, stooped man in kilts, the legendary Scots entertainer, appeared, waving a shillelagh. After a few congratulatory words, accompanied by a bagpiper, he regaled us with "I Love a Lassie, "Roamin' in the Gloamin'," "Just a Wee Deoch and Doris," and "End of the Road." Thousands joined in. He seemed the essence of Scotland. As he prepared to leave the stage, the shattering yells of the audience drew him back for encores. He was more alert to the joyous occasion than he had been when I'd seen him months before in England.

The next morning, much hung-over, we left Edinburgh for Paris and the final two days of our leave.

On our second evening in Paris, Marlene Dietrich was scheduled for a concert in a large theater. Most soldiers knew "Lili Marlene" by heart, an amazing song for wartime since it crossed all national boundaries. Dietrich sang it in Africa, Sicily, and throughout Europe, always before enthralled soldiers. Though a German national, she was entirely loyal to America and the Allied cause. Postponing her stunning career, she dedicated herself to the Allied troops. She was often under fire, riding in jeeps, motorcycles, and even hiking to reach GI audiences. She made recordings for the Office of Strategic Services, the U. S. propaganda arm, of popular American songs in German, which were broadcast to the Reich over underground radio. Among the songs were: "Annie Doesn't Live Here Anymore," "The Surrey With the Fringe On Top," "Taking a Chance on Love," and "I Couldn't Sleep A Wink Last Night."

"Lili Marlene," her signature ballad, moved soldiers on both sides of the war for its tale of the soldier who leaves his girl, knowing that she will be fickle. He fears dying in battle, a possibility that seems imманent, and by recalling his first meeting with Lili in the lamplight outside his barracks, their shadows melting into one as she kissed him, he palliates his loss by vowing eternal love. The simple lyrics with their intermittent march cadences and tremulous romantic modulations struck universal depths of love, loss, desperate waiting, and a resolve that stirred men far from home, confronting death.

I discovered Dietrich in high school when I bought a 78 album of her songs, and, although I did not understand German, I played them repeatedly on a windup Victrola. Hers was the only album I owned. These records, fragile, revolving seventy-eight times per minute, smelled of the shellac of which they were made. They held no more than half a dozen ballads. You wiped them frequently to remove fingerprints and dust affecting the quality of the play. A friend, a Wagnerite who had loaned me his *Ring* cycle, on a fat album of 78s, had recommended her. I also saw her films *The Blue Angel, Destry Rides Again,* and *Kismet,* and was so entranced I paid scant attention to the plot or to the other stars.

I was drawn to her throaty octaves and to her peculiar humor which, in the films, kept men at bay and was tinged with masculinity. Her elegance was like that of an Ionic column, fluted, contained, and pure. Also, particularly in *Blue Angel,* there were lesbian overtones. By appearing inaccessible, she could flaunt sexuality (as she did, painted gold, in the campy dance scene from *Kismet*) and at the same time seem aloof from it, almost as though she were impersonating Dietrich. I loved this androgyne.

During the walk to the theater, as we neared the Place de l'Opera, we joined a crowd gathered around Bob Hope, Frances Langford, and Jerry Colonna. The trio was trying to enter a limousine parked at a hotel. Hope was contemptuous of the crowd composed largely of GIs, the servicemen he supposedly loved. He vexatiously refused to respond to any questions or to give autographs. He bullied his way to the car, cursing. I had always mistrusted Hope, so was not surprised by his behavior. My negative estimate of him has never changed.

To see Dietrich, we waited in line for over three hours. A halcyon summer evening. A dozen GIs were already there when we reached the theater.

When the doors opened, Bill and I raced forwards, claiming seats front and center, first row. The hall was soon filled with men seated in the aisles and standing to the rear. The house lights dimmed to a pale rose blended with lavender. A hush. Theme music from a reedy orchestra—"Falling in Love Again." A spotlight low on a red curtain, the only illumination in the darkened house. The curtain parted slightly, and to uproarious applause one curvaceous leg appeared, svelte and silk-shod, followed shortly by the complete Dietrich in a silver lamé gown. She held an unlighted cigarette in a long white holder and wore white gloves. Her shoulder-length blonde hair was immaculate. Her face was the exact image we had seen in her films— the plucked eyebrows, the sculpted cheek bones, the sexy lips.

She opened with "See What The Boys In The Back-Room Will Have," one of her most popular hits. The half-spoken, half-sung lyrics sounded velvety. During the famous tremolo of the refrain "and tell them I cried," she jostled her voice box by shaking her throat with her fingers, producing an odd bleat. Her humor was fluted and subtle, suggestive and toned. Her moves were minimal; her arm and hand gestures restrained.

In the cabaret songs "Johnny" and "Peter," her voice, scratchy with pain, was slightly off-key. At other times, sexy and caressing, she sang from shadows, the broken English adding to the mystique. In "I'm the Laziest Gal In Town," one of her funniest songs, she jibed at herself. If she weren't lazy, perhaps she wouldn't be so lonely. In her heart-"achin' " state, she craved for her dude to "bring home the bacon." She relished the funky end-rhyme. Whether the "bacon" is the man's penis or the money he'll fetch doesn't much matter.

"Lili Marlene" produced pandemonium. She stopped, bowed, and raised a white gloved arm to quiet the audience. Dietrich *was* Lili. I locked the stream of her sound in my ear and cried. By evoking such immense love and beauty, performing in a city that was itself a monument to the human spirit (both Allies and Nazis vowed not to bomb it), with most of Europe in ruins, Dietrich asserted all that remained constant and fine.

On receiving boquets of roses she moved slowly around the stage and, with the orchestra playing "Falling In Love Again," she threw flowers at us, kissing each rose before she flung it. The applause was rapturous. We were all standing, facing the stage.

In mid-September, 1945, I was promoted to tech 5, a non-combatant corporal's rank. By the end of October, our unit had completed its work in France. We were now an army of occupation. Cadre were sent to a variety of replacement depots and regular units. New orders sent me to Compiègne southeast of Paris, near the forest made famous by the signing of the treaty concluding World War I, so humiliating to the Germans. Hitler's first major act on conquering France was to bring the French leaders to that same carriage for a demeaning treaty.

En route to Compiègne, we settled for a week in one of Cardinal Richelieu's palaces near Paris, now much run-down and utilized mainly for temporarily housing Allied troops. Groups of four or five men were assigned to rooms used by servants during the Cardinal's tenure. The main building was a massive rectangle of three sides, opening on an esplanade of fountains and gardens leading to a broad vista terminating near a forest. Fountains were clogged, and the gardens nearest the palace were overrun with mildewed roses gone wild. A few large trout swam in a pond; it led to a sluice that emptied into a stream flowing through the estate. Though run-down, the palace still exuded much formal elegance. In an attic I found a scrap of parchment dating from the seventeenth century; it seemed to deal with some legal matter. A spot of red sealing wax was affixed. I kept it, fetching it back to the States, naively assuming that once translated it would resolve some vexed matter of ancient French history. It turned out to be worth nothing, a paper for a minor land deal.

At Compiègne we billeted in a four-story mansion on the outskirts, one with a facade of quoins in an Italian Renaissance style. Incoming troops, on their way to replenish units in occupied Germany, were housed further out at a former French military base. My duties were essentially what they had been in Troyes—to assist the sergeant-major, Pete Winslow, a burly, civilized, fortyish midwesterner who loved opera and his pipe. He had bushy graying eyebrows and tufts of hair in his ears. Being on his staff was like being in civilian life. His acolyte was a doe-eyed youngster from rural Illinois, Bill Black. Black shared a room with me near Pete's quarters, and the three of us would sit for hours talking, joking, and playing 500 rummy. Black looked younger than his actual years. His ruddy cheeks and small mouth gave him a feminine appearance. We called him "Shirley Temple." We became almost inseparable, so much so that other men speculated that we were lovers. Black spoke often of the girl he would marry when he returned to De Kalb.

We had the services of a gaunt, horse-faced maid who often wept, regaling us with fears that her husband would arrive at any moment to kill her—he suspected her of sleeping with Germans. Not true, she declared! Over the weeks, she built up such a picture of this monster that when he actually arrived we found a thoroughly meek, short, mousey man. He leaned against an entrance column beneath a fractured urn which once held geraniums, waiting for her. Wearing a flimsy purple dress buttoned at the throat, wiping her hands on her muslin apron, she walked up to him, raised her fist, and began railing. She excoriated him most of the morning, eventually moving her scene to her private quarters. The clamor was so intense that the first sergeant, to rid us of the pair, gave her two days off.

Apart from walks through the Compiègne Forest and along the boulevards leading into the city, and trips to Chateau-Thierry, I remained at the villa helping to process hundreds of soldiers passing through to occupy German cities. The "other" war in Asia seemed remote, as it had all along. On July 16th, the first atomic bomb, produced at Los Alamos, New Mexico, exploded at Almogordo in the New Mexican desert. Despite some saber rattling, intended to intimidate the Japanese, we never guessed that Truman would actually drop a bomb. Yet, on August 6, a U. S. Army Air Force B-20, the Enola Gay, dropped its load on Hiroshima. Three days later, the Russians declared war on Japan, invading Manchuria and northern Korea. On that same morning, the United States demolished Nagasaki. On September 7, aboard the battleship Missouri, anchored in Tokyo Bay, a formal treaty of surrender was signed. On the 9th, General Douglas MacArthur was appointed supreme commander of Japan. In mid-September, our Replacement Depot moved to Mosbach, Germany, eighteen miles south of Heidelberg, the famous university town. Black and Winslow received orders to return to the States. Promoted to T/Sgt., I was now in charge of the headquarters office. I looked forward to Germany.

5

Germany: September 1945–April 1946

MOSBACH lies on the Neckar River, about twenty miles south-east of Heidelberg. This sizeable yet rural town emerged from the war physically unscathed, of no interest to Allied bombers as a munitions or supply center. Among picturesque half-timbered houses stand newer buildings in the fascist style dating from the thirties. These have plain stucco fronts, are designed as boxes perforated with unadorned windows, and occasionally boast steep hip roofs.

Our headquarters was in one of Mosbach's few steam-heated buildings, a three-story stucco edifice once inhabited by an insurance company. The ground floor contained our offices; living quarters were on the upper floors. As sergent-major I enjoyed a large bedroom and a sitting room with bevelled mirrors, French doors, reading lamps, and high-backed, sturdy, brown leather furniture decorated with brass studs. I also had a radio, which was always tuned to the Armed Forces Network's music and news. My window faced a tree-filled park on the Neckar and a cemetery filled with roughly-hewn, Wagnerian stone monuments, most of them to slain soldiers. These stele appeared to have had a single designer. All were of dark granite, monolithic, suggestive of massive, but broken, human bodies appropriate for a *Götterdämmerung*. Each was graced by weeping willows.

Our officers were billeted in the town center, in another steam-heated building, one much larger than ours, which held both a fancy club for officers and an enlisted men's mess hall. The latter, converted from what was formerly a beer *stube*, had low-arched ceilings decorated with vines, leaves, and cornucopias of fruit and grain and insipidly

In my room, Mosbach.

smiling cherubs garbed in ribbons of pastel plaster. Most of the officers had German mistresses who worked in the dining rooms and on the janitorial staff. There was a tacit pecking order: the more prestigious the woman's job, the more advanced the rank of her paramour. Colonel McKinley, the commanding officer, enjoyed the classiest female of all, a svelte, bright creature adept in English and secretarial work who wore her long blonde hair parted straight across her scalp and twisted in a pair of long, Heidiesque braids down her back.

As I marched the men through the streets to breakfast at 6 a.m., I counted cadence loudly, commanding the men to "Sound Off," which was inconsiderate of the sleeping officers. Lieutenant Redfern, a dark man with a huge nose, sloppy breasts, and a querulous voice, who was in charge of the officers' quarters, insisted that we approach the place

71

In Mosbach, Germany, 1946.

Calling the detachment to order, 1946.

quietly. We despised Redfern as a toadying officers' gofer. We continued counting raucous cadences as we traversed the cobblestones, disturbing the officers snuggled up with their doxies in goose-feather beds. Redfern, vexed, insisting that I salute him, gave me "a direct order" to "have your men tiptoe if they must." If the noise persisted "measures would be taken."

The next morning, as we approached the three-storied, creamcolored building, I shouted to the men: "Let's have quiet as we approach this fucking mess hall. The officers' whores need their sleep." Redfern, waiting with fists clenched, ordered me to follow him into a vestibule off the dining room. Behind a pair of French doors, livid, he threatened to "bust" me for insubordination. Declaring that I had not heard "the end of this," Redfern spun around, and without looking back disappeared up a stairs. The men joked about the episode; yet, to avoid further trouble, from that point on, we approached the mess hall quietly. Redfern always received my morning salute.

Despite my stubbornness over Redfern, I found giving orders difficult, and in using my authority counted on the support of other NCOs. I could request work details of them without having to give a direct order myself. The most supportive NCOs were Tom Skehan, the sergeant in charge of all rosters and reports; his assistant Danny Jackson, a lanky youth from Dallas; Stacy Bills, a North Carolinian, in charge of liaisons between the units scattered about Mosbach that processed troops on their way to military government units elsewhere in Germany; and John Ulicni, from Chicago, the morning reports clerk. Increasingly, our primary function was to process men returning to the States for discharge. With the pressures of war over we engaged in much horse play once our regular duties were performed.

Earlier, while stationed in Compiègne, France, during the first sergeant's absences on furlough, when I was temporarily in charge, I sensed the fact of power almost guarantees that your orders will be effectuated. Having my fourth stripe also helped. Still, I was never completely easy when faced with personal confrontations. When a soldier committing some breach appeared I would rehearse myself, anticipating what might transpire, "scripting," in other words, the possibilities. I would take deep breaths, emptying my diaphragm so that my voice would be resonant. I tried to avoid preachy tones. Once a difficult soldier appeared my voice would betray my timidity if I hesitated before speaking. Particularly difficult were offenders who had been derelict on duty. Always, of course, Major McKinney, the CO, had the final say, and in tough cases I would dismiss the culprit and recommend action by the major.

Some of the men had drinking problems, which I sought to alleviate through counseling, never with much success. One troubled soldier was Rudy McKinny, whose mother had located him through the Red Cross, after hearing nothing from her son for two years. Her inquiry reached my desk. I had suspected that Rudy was illiterate, and as he stood before me, short and nervous, his red hair plastered to his scalp, he confessed that all he could do was sign his name. He sat down and together we wrote to his mother. "Pretend you are talking to her," I said. As he spoke his laborious words, I wrote them. He signed his name. Jerry Slocum's problem was different. About to go home, he discovered a venereal drip. He feared telling his wife. "There *must* be a drug," he said, near tears. He had lapsed only once, with a whore in Metz, on his way to Mosbach. I sent him for consultation to a military hospital in Heidelberg.

With peace, an ebullience prevailed which I first sensed in France after the victory in Europe, and particularly after the bombings of Hiroshima and Nagasaki. We looked forward to going home. The question was not *if* but how soon. We drank more than ever, both in our rooms and at the Enlisted Men's Club, a sizeable former restaurant and beer hall managed by Germans. Three or four nights a week we assembled, drinking hard booze and American beer, sheltered beneath the shadowy, smoky interior of coves and low arches adorned with vines and pastel murals of vineyards. Tom Skehan played honky-tonk piano, pounding out sentimental Irish ballads and favorites from Grable, Hayworth, and Faye movies. No matter how much he drank, he was always clear-headed, regaling us with his Irish humor. He was stocky, of medium height, and had a delicious acerbic wit. For example, he would deliver cutting jibes against some stupid action of the CO. Trained in music, he had a cultured aura, which was special in that heterogenous gathering of men from assorted backwashes of American life. The German waitresses played up to him (and us), expecting cigarettes, chocolate, and coffee.

We spent much time on our uniforms. We belled our trousers over the buckled boot tops so that the sharp creases would fall exactly so. Our shirts, too, were immaculately creased, the ubiquitous tan tie carefully arranged. The Eisenhower jackets (we never appeared in the streets without them) fit our waists snugly. We usually left one pair of combat boots with a cobbler for polishing (we supplied the polish). Daily, I led the company in calisthenics on the tarmac in front of our headquarters. My coal-black hair I brushed into a pompadour.

Though Mosbach was staunchly Roman Catholic, there was a Lutheran church for Protestants. We dove-tailed our weekly services with the Germans. The facade was high-pitched, half-timbered, and displayed a gray stone image of Christ crucified above a Romanesque-style portal. The vaulted interior, redolent of incense and burned wax, had an ornate carved wooden altar adorned with a gold sunburst accentuating another image of Christ. The image was nude except for a swirl of painted wood carved like ribbon candy floating over the loins. The downcast face had a sad late adolescent look and rouged cheeks. Drops of purplish blood dripped from iron thorns around the head. The entire image tilted, as though it would float off at any moment. The ends of the pews were decorated with tamarack and spruce boughs and dried flowers.

My last Christmas in Europe was bittersweet, for a number of friends were going home. Bill departed after the New Year. There was a pattern, one we observed on rosters of names passing through Mosbach on their way to ships in Le Havre or Brest, a pattern shaped by dates of enlistment. Skehan and I were both inducted in March, 1943; April seemed about right for our exit. With luck we would sail on the same ship.

We seldom talked about our futures. Few of us had clear goals, other than getting on with our lives. Returning to the civilian jobs we left was guaranteed, though I did not much relish being a file clerk for an insurance company the rest of my life. Tom could always enter the family beer-distribution business; that would depend on the wishes of his wife, a painter, who urged him to complete his education and become a psychiatrist. He saw his music as a hobby rather than a career.

There was a vague chance that I might go to college, for I revered books, even fantasized writing them. Although I knew that writers kept journals, I lacked the discipline, diverting those energies into letters written home at least twice a week, often more. I kept half a dozen Army-issue paperbacks, mainly biographies of historical figures and a couple of novels, on my bed-side table; none of these did I read past the first fifty pages. I never liked mysteries, westerns, or romances, seeing them as a waste of time. I was intimidated by the thought of a university, and was ignorant even of how one applied. My image of campus life came from films, primarily from Jack Benny's "Charley's Aunt" and from Jack Okie and Joe E. Brown features. Despite the enticement of the G. I. Bill, I persisted in feeling that advanced education was for the rich; I would be out of place. The only novels I read from cover to cover were Henry Miller's *Tropic of Cancer* and *Tropic of Capricorn.* These famous Olympia paperbacks I bought at a Seine bookstall in Paris. On many evenings, smashed on schnapps and GI pineapple juice, we read portions aloud. I had no idea there were so many sexual positions. My favorite episode featured an irrepressible Miller screwing a woman who sat in his lap on a swing. Major McKinley asked to see the novels. Alas, he later claimed someone stole them from his room. He lied.

We assumed the war was just. The Japs and Germans were enemies of civilization. And we were hostile towards conscientious objectors. Lew Ayers, star of the Oscar-winning "All Quiet On The Western Front," deserved blacklisting as a CO. We despised 4Fs as shirkers who had conned their draft boards. And Jeanette Rankin, the single Congressperson voting against declaring war on Japan and Germany, struck us as dotty and irresponsible, possibly a traitor. Some of our hostility arose from envy; most of us would have opted not to serve if we had a legitimate excuse. Moreover, our extreme youth and naivete explained our accepting the propaganda films of our early training. We were encouraged to think, if we thought at all, in tabloid fashion and to trust our superiors—the NCOs and particularly the officers. We were trained to follow orders, never to speculate for ourselves. Further, risking our lives made more sense if the war made sense; to have doubted might have generated cowardice, increasing the chances of death for those actually in battle.

We did read *Stars and Stripes*, for its cartoons and features and not for battlefront news. Weekly information and education sessions, conducted by officers and NCOs supposedly informed on national and international trends, were poorly attended. As the top NCO at Mosbach, I never required my men to appear, something Major McKinley complained of. When I said that the meetings were a waste, he agreed but insisted that it was my duty to encourage attendance. The I&E people could then feel useful. Most of the latter were poorly trained, and the few meetings I sat through deteriorated into bull sessions with the audience hooting and shouting at these "experts." To most GIs, I&E types were fuckups at normal military jobs. Most of their "information" on international affairs was culled from the New York *Herald Tribune*, Paris edition.

The Germans, deprived of nearly every amenity, threatened with starvation, and mourning loved ones still missing weeks after the cessation of the war, faced a new Christmas. In one shop, an old craftsman carved jumping jacks, which he left unpainted since no paint was available, delineating faces and clothes with a burnisher. He filled his window with the stringed toys. I bought one for my sister Jane. Shops in town were decorated with wreaths of fir boughs adorned with cones and berries. Old creches appeared, as did balsam and spruce trees trimmed with ornaments and wax candles. Bakeries, lacking sugar, jam, dates, and raisins for cakes and tarts, sold bread cut and twisted into trees, candy canes, and dolls. Occasional hare of goose paté, the latter complete with glazed feet and heads, appeared in shop windows. Seasonal greeting cards, retrieved from past caches, were great favorites, and we snapped them up. Our headquarters published cards featuring black and white German photographs of branches heaped with snow, of chicadees and picturesque villages deep in wintry landscapes. On Christmas Eve day we hosted a party for over one hundred

Our company Christmas tree, Mosbach, December 1945.

children, serving strawberry punch, elaborate Christmas cakes, cookies, and ice cream. Each child received a stocking of candy and fruit.

On Christmas Eve, a joint service for Germans and Americans occurred at midnight in the Lutheran church. Skehan, Robertson, and I took a pew near the oak pulpit which soared above us like the prow of a stage-set frigate. A huge eagle carved from chestnut supported a buckram Bible and grasped holly berries in its claws. The local pastor and our chaplain (in uniform) shared the service. Mimeographed carols were printed in both English and German. A spruce, hung with wood and woven straw ornaments, and lighted with wax tapers, reached well up into the rafters, exuding light and odor. Rich shadows flickered on the whitewashed stone and high over the vaulted ribs of the ceiling. Deposits of frost and snow crested the outside of the multi-paned windows, scintillating with candle light, trembling the icy crystals.

Carols swelled, sung first in German, then in English. The life-sized Christ over the altar, carved of purple wood, with head slumped, seemed to bless us, prescient that all human lives were paradigms of His life—fulfillment, containment, brutalization, pain, and, most incredibly, of final triumph. I ached loving my Savior and the men who were sharing my life. And I ached for home.

In Wisconsin it was three in the afternoon, in Mosbach nearly midnight. "Silent Night" concluded the service. German pastor and American chaplain embraced. We turned to the Germans, shook hands, and filed out into the crisp, snowy night.

Back in quarters, we drank cognac and sang more carols. At noon the next day, a feast complete with printed menu was served. We ate turkey and all the trimmings, pumpkin pie and ice cream, coffee and cognac. The mess sergeant, a muscular man with a cleft chin and azure eyes, resembled a short William Holden. He made a point of stopping at each table. He was proud of his German cooks, he said, and had given them bonuses of turkey and tins of coffee. His mistress, a lithe brunette about a foot taller than he, supervised the waitresses with snaps of authority. Today, however, she smilingly dashed about, ordering more coffee here, more pie there. Each waitress wore a cluster of mistletoe tied with candy cane ribbon. We lingered over the cognac and coffee. There were cigars. Even Lieutenant Redfern, who had received his orders to return to San Francisco, was benign.

One warm, late February morning a motor pool truck drove us to Heidelberg, twenty miles north of Mosbach. The driver would return to headquarters around midnight. We followed the Neckar River which twisted and churned like a fast-moving stream along the route. In the city itself, a minor industrial center, no bomb damage was visible, although we understood that small factories and houses in the northern suburbs were destroyed. Most older buildings, of a pinkish stone, gave a fairy-tale aura. At the university no students were visible; the Allied military government had not given permission for classes and seminars to resume, and, in fact, housed a headquarters there.

With Tom Skehan, I climbed Philosopher's Walk which ran above the university and offered extensive views of the campus and of the town. Here, below enormous romantic firs and beeches so thick that the floor was lavish with bronze leaves and needles, great philosophers, scientists, and writers had walked, meditating, smoking meerschaums, exchanging views on issues of life and destiny. Much of the intellectual shape of Europe was fashioned here. Although I knew none of these worthies, I felt reverential. Tom mentioned Fichte and Hegel, and he had read Immanuel Kant. "Lots of moonshine," he observed. "Things like categorical imperatives meant to improve our lives. Can't see much evidence that they worked." He laughed under his breath. "But you, Peters, you're taken in by all this, right?" I confessed that I was. I was a fledgling poet complete with beret, bohemian smock, and flowing cravat. If I were patient, during a rosy dusk, inspiration would seize me, racing me back to my attic garret where I would scribble a masterpiece.

Heidelberg itself was crammed with GIs jostling and whistling at frauleins. Eventually Tom and I spotted a beer hall, an ancient cellar, crowded with both Germans and Americans. The mingling was rare, for in Mosbach we did not fraternize. Here honey-colored, highly varnished tables accommodated a dozen or more drinkers. Harried waitresses, clad in Bavarian aprons decorated with tiny flowers, most resembling blonde Heidis complete with pigtails, served enormous schooners of beer and trays of pretzels. The Germans linked arms and, still seated, shouted drinking songs while they pulled first to the right and then to the left, stopping only for more beer and pounding the tables. Knowing little German, I had no idea what they sang. Shortly, in compensation, we began singing, though without ever attaining the force of the Germans: "Roll her over in the clover and do it again,"

"Mademoiselle from Armentieres," "There's a long, long trail a winding." Shortly before midnight, drunk, we sang all the way back to Mosbach where we fell into our beds.

Since Mosbach was far enough south to be fairly temperate, by the second week of March spring arrived. I had never seen so many forsythia. Willows all over town shot forth. Jonquils and tulips appeared, and geraniums kept indoors during the winter now flourished in window boxes and outdoor planters. Those Germans who managed to husband a few potatoes, dug garden plots. Some planted old cabbage, turnip, and carrot seeds. Dandelions grew everywhere; the leaves were harvested and eaten during the brief season before they turned bitter. The blossoms were gathered for wine. Apple, cherry, and plum trees were in bloom.

Frauleins waited tables and tended bar in the Enlisted Men's Club near headquarters. The two-story club was in the fascist style, gray unadorned stucco with harsh corner and roof angles and plain windows that seemed to have no sills, flush with the exterior walls. Only on the ground floor was there any space for window boxes. Though built as a restaurant, the place was so subdued you could walk by without realizing it was there. Since the street was elevated, you stepped down to reach the modest, black front door which seemed more appropriate for a single-family dwelling that a public place. A low-ceilinged, unadorned room was amply appointed with a large area for dancing and another section filled with simple wooden tables and chairs. Near the front door, clear of furniture, German women, invited by the management, made assignations with GIs. Having agreed on a tryst, it was easy for the pair to slip out unnoticed. Such trafficking was, of course, illegal. For the frauleins, a GI paramour meant nylons, cigarettes, chocolate, and coffee. The club was open from mid-afternoon until three in the morning.

I was pretty sure which GIs indulged. Most talked a good line. Occasionally my buddies teased me for being celibate. Often, in bed, I would fantasize about females, particularly their breasts, as a way of inducing sleep. No matter how luscious, these images segued into males. Lanky, well-proportioned, sandy-haired Danny Jackson often appeared. When I heard rumors that he was having an affair in another detachment, I was jealous, and whenever he came into my office to secure some file I would undress him, knowing that if I ever responded

81

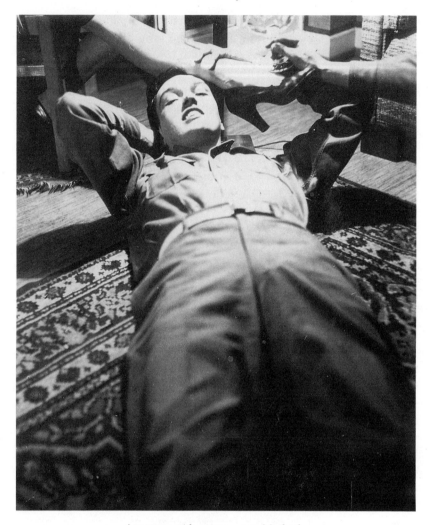

At a party with army nurses, Mosbach.

to his signs (one day he snapped a ruler at a semi-hardon flowing beneath his trousers) I would back off. I was ignorant of real sex with either men and women and was secure only with my own masturbatory fantasies. I dreaded that the CO might order me to investigate Jackson as a "queer," and "undesirable." If that happened, my rational self would follow orders, even if it meant a dishonorable discharge. What a hypocrite! While I hungered for Jackson, I felt self-hatred and vowed to God that I would never sin again. Meeting Giesela helped.

Giesela Wiessner was eighteen, slender, full-breasted, red-haired, and spoke English with a mere trace of an accent. At the club she served wine. Though I preferred beer and spirits, I looked forward to sitting at her bar.

"How are you tonight?" I'd ask.

"I'm very good. And you?" She wore no rings or bracelets. Her only adornment was an ovate pendant, ruby red, on a slim gold chain around her neck, containing in its center a white rose and a white bud.

"That's beautiful." I pointed to the pendant.

She held it towards me. "It is very old in my family. A, how do you say it, a *gift* from my great-grandfather to my great-grandmother at their engagement."

I stroked the silky stone with my thumb.

"I will never put it aside." She brushed a stray lock of hair from her face. "You understand? I want everything to be pleasant."

"Yes," I said.

She served wine to another GI.

"Where would you rather be right now?" I asked when she returned.

"Walking with you under beech trees. Their leaves drop so thick they make no noise." She paused. "There'd be no war," she said.

During temperate, late-winter days of weak sun, the fields lay white and bare, and the remote snowy mountains were tinted mauve. We usually strolled hand-in-hand, silently. Occasionally, I would practice German words, assembling an olio of nouns with little sense of the grammar. As a result, I felt stupid, as though a German had memorized a thousand boxed English name cards, most of them for concrete objects. I perpetually confused genders.

By late February, our excursions followed a routine, Giesela preferring to leave the town to the south where she would be least apt to be recognized. When I challenged her she'd say that once we Americans withdrew, having fraternized would make it difficult for her to marry a local man. "You don't understand this, do you? Men are not alike; I mean, women find it more difficult, both inside and outside a war. German women understand." She paused. "My family will like you. It's the gossips in the village."

I embraced her. We were standing on a narrow, gravel-strewn path leading down to a small, reed-filled lake with a crude dock built of fir logs.

"I'm not special," she said. "I am quite, how would you say it, ordinary. Like you, I lived on a farm. The Nazis took it from us, for they said it was producing too little food. They took my father and brothers for the army and moved the rest of us here to Mosbach. I am not gifted, though I am young. This is very serious, I feel."

"Don't say that." I gave a nervous laugh.

"Everything is so green now. Is Wisk-konsin so green?" She paused. "Under this green there's rotting, which I don't like. Smell it." She kicked at some mulch, scattering the leaves, then knelt, drawing me down beside her. "See?" The soil in her hand smelled like souring liver. "My country will have to change."

She broke away and sat on a log thrust out into the lake. A fish gulping for a fly broke the surface, fluttering the water in concentric rings. Giesela rested her chin on her knees and stared at the water. "I miss my two brothers and father greatly," she said. "Have they escaped the Russians? Are they wandering with shoe-soles flapping, coming home? I don't know. Perhaps they are dead."

I wanted to soothe her. "I'm sorry" was the best I could manage, feeling gauche.

One of her favorite stops was at an uncle's farm, one that remained productive and, hence, had pleased the Nazis. The uncle, in his late forties, a consumptive, was excused from military service. His lungs, Giesela explained, were sodden masses choked with blood. Even if he had had the money, there were no antibiotics for civilians, and the hospitals were turned into recovery wards for injured German soldiers.

I never actually met the uncle. Seeing us approach, he would disappear into the barn before we had barely entered the farm yard, which was strewn with slush, cow manure, soaked straw, and noisy gatherings of chickens and geese. I would spy him bent over working, wearing a faded brown corduroy jacket and pants, and a visored woolen cap pulled down over his ears.

Giesela's aunt, a plump, short woman with a red face splotched with veins, was effusive. She would wipe her meaty hands on her begrimed apron and invite us in. Her wooden shoes were bespattered with soil. Heavy worsted socks, lavish with holes, reached her knees. She moved about her spacious kitchen, occasionally holding one palm of her hand against her lower back, as a gesture that her arthritis was getting worse. The farmhouse itself was low with whitewashed stone walls a foot thick. For generations, a lethal damp crippled the woman locked within those walls. The aunt knew no English, so would chatter in German to Giesela, anxious for family news. She had three sons; two had disappeared on the eastern front, the third, a sailor, died on a submarine in the North Atlantic.

In the crowded room, Giesela's mother, two adolescent brothers, and the farm aunt with her two teen-aged daughters, all seated around a long oak table, awaited me. I carried gifts—a large tin of cherry jam, two pounds of coffee, and chocolate bars. Giesela's mother was wearing a dark blue, crepe dress with a shirred skirt and a blouse with a ruffled neck and cuffs. Her fawn-colored hair was drawn back into a bun secured with a mother-of-pearl comb.

The general introductions, managed by Giesela, were accompanied by tittering from the youngsters. Mrs. Wiessner placed my gifts at her end of the table.

"The food is ready," Giesela said. "It's my mother's best soup, of pork with egg yolks beaten into it. Pepper. Salt. Onion. All it will lack is a good lemon." She gestured to a chair. "There's where you are meant to sit," she said.

The soup was served from a ceramic tureen in the shape of a goose with a notched top and a ladle. Round loaves of fresh, dark bread, quartered, appeared. "Let's open the tin of cherry jam," Giesela said, rising. Soup bowls and small plates were decorated with roses. The flatware was of silver. They must have hidden it from the authorities during the war.

"The schools are not yet open," Giesela said. The brothers were in their early teens, and both had close-cropped reddish hair and freckles. Though slim, the older boy was already filling out. They wore blue shirts and faded gabardine trousers. "Rot and Klimt are so bored," Giesela said, "for in town there is little to do. If we only had our farm . . ." She pointed behind her to a shelf covered with an embroidered doily and an assortment of pictures. "That is my father," she explained. "Those at his sides are my brothers." A third photo of another soldier she did not identify.

Suddenly the mother, in broken English, said: "Hitler was to blame. Are you German? Hitler destroyed us."

"Yes," I replied, "but I am also Irish, a mix."

"Hitler lived in *Österreich*," she continued. *"Er war nicht deutsch."*

She rattled on with Giesela interpreting: "She says that before America was in the war, you Americans liked our country. You could

85

have fought on our side. She also said that America and Germany could have ruled the world. Now, all we have is misery, while you have happiness."

Mrs. Wiessner arose to make coffee. I asked Giesela to distribute the chocolate; there were enough bars for everyone.

"Klimt wants to know," Giesela said, "if you have killed anyone in this war."

"No. I have been lucky."

The boy was silent. I had no idea what he felt. Did he think I might have shot his father and brothers?

Giesela said that we must leave, for she was working that evening.

"Be kind to my Giesela," Mrs. Wiessner said, shaking my hand. "Do not harm her."

Arm in arm we walk through the quiet town. Two widows wearing mannish felt hats, each trailing a pheasant feather, walk home from the cemetery. A gaggle of youths and girls lean over a stone bridge, flirting. An old man burdened with saplings for brooms passes. A mongrel investigates scents at door sills.

We reach a bakery shop. "In a few hours we'll have our Monday morning bread." Giesela's smile is both affectionate and sad. She lingers. "Are you ever a window? One very emptied?"

"What a strange question."

"My family likes you." She pauses. "I want to say more, Bob, of that picture, the third one, in the living room." She tightens her collar. "That was Kurt's. We were to marry last year. His family farm lived near ours."

"Where is he now?"

"Disappeared in Russia, like so many others. The last word from him was last October."

The club juke box is blaring. Through the frosty windows we see men milling about. Activity on Sunday begins earlier than on other evenings.

"I will leave you here. I can't be late to work."

We embrace.

"Tonight I will visit your room, Bob, if you'd like that."

Shortly after midnight, as we slip into the building, the NCO on duty gives a cheery greeting. Upstairs, I hang Giesela's coat behind the door.

Her dress is of two-toned, brown satin with a dark bodice and skirt. A tan, silky material, fringed, covers her bosom.

"I didn't expect a soldier's room to be so nice," she says, taking a glass of wine.

The room is a stark off-white. The only decorative notes are a pair of sepia reproductions of smiling waifs proffering flowers to a farmer with a team of oxen. I have intended to replace them with something more original, but the pictures come with the rooms, and I am used to them; in fact, most of the time I don't even notice them.

"I'm glad you're here," I say. I sit on the bed. Giesela sets her wine glass down. "You are hiding your thoughts," she says, taking my hand.

"I didn't think you would come," I say.

"Do be careful," she asks.

I nervously loosen her brassiere. Her breasts maintain their plumpness. I cup them in my hands, then move my fingers over the nipples, kissing them. The flow of skin towards Giesela's abdomen, milk white, is traced with lilac veins. A moist warmth. I fold back the blankets and douse the light. A street lamp provides a diminished glow.

Giesela lies back. We kiss and she unbuttons my shirt, freeing it from my trousers. I brush her eyes with my lips. Her mouth, slightly ajar, invites my tongue. I sluff my trousers and shorts, and she grabs me, caressing me. We roll over. Her nipples graze my mouth. Her body presses mine. I slip easily inside her. Her contractions nearly induce ejaculation. I withdraw. "Is it all right?" I ask. "Does it hurt?"

I thrust more vigorously, pumping, pumping, grasping her. My brain feels bifurcated. For a flash Mike Swenson in Paris is lying beneath me. I am about to explode between his thighs. I can smell his musk. "Giesela," I murmur. "Giesela." I kiss her throat and come, collapsing, with lips ajar. Strands of her damp hair are in my mouth. Then she stiffens. "Bob," she says, trying to get free. "Bob, I'm bleeding."

I turn on the light. Her thighs are red. I have blood on my legs. I hold her, drawing the blankets up. "You'll be fine," I say, caressing her face. But I am frightened.

"I didn't know this would come, the bleeding, I mean. I wanted it to be so good."

"It was good, Giesela. It was good."

Using the sheet, I wipe the blood and assist her to the bath. The blood lessens. I clean myself. Later I make tea with lemon. Giesela sips slowly. "I should go home now," she says. "My mother always worries."

"I shall walk with you," I say, helping her on with her coat.

Returning to my room, I put the soiled sheets in the bathtub to soak, remake my bed, open the window for cool air, pour some cognac, and sit in the over-stuffed chair thinking. The cognac down my throat is a ribbon of hot light. Was the evening a success? But why did Mike appear? We had never had sex, unless our simply sleeping together in the small bed after the whore had quit our Paris hotel qualified.

I gaze at veins traversing the back of my hand, rising from the knobby area where the wrist joins the arm and disappears below the knuckles. One vein, dominant, ripples diagonally across the ulna, forking into yet another vein which lacks much of a sense of either source or destination.

Three men who shared personal histories with me, Bert Siever, Bill Turney, and Mike Clark, all feared failures with women, and they had failures. Most men, it appears, erect barriers, afraid of losing face with the "weaker sex," opening themselves up to ridicule, or worse—your partner might think you're "queer." The brain's switch for "go" ignores "caution."

Warmed by the cognac, I crave to see Giesela again, even fantasizing that she will marry me and live in Wisconsin. Without removing my clothes, I fall asleep, and in a vivid dream return to Paris with Siever, where I replay our assignation with the whore. This time Siever is the file clerk Danny Jackson! I wake up shouting; it takes nearly an hour to fall back to sleep.

I sleep until nearly noon, rise, shower, have lunch with the men, and spend the day catching up on memoranda for Major McKinley. The major is casual about regular hours. He himself seldom reports for duty until after lunch, "an officer's prerogative," he calls it. "I trust you'll keep things flying, sergeant." He is negotiating for his return home to Seattle and appears at my desk to see if his latest memo to higher authorities is ready for his signature.

"Jackson is typing it," I tell him. "He'll have it in a few minutes."

"Good," he says. "I hope to get in some golf today." He is about to enter his office when he returns to my desk. "This is confidential," he says. "But there are rumors about Jackson. Keep your eye on him, and let me know if anything untoward is going on." He pauses. "We've got to be on top," he advises. "No perverts here. Nothing can stop my going home."

"Yes, sir," I say.

"Here's the CO's letter," says Jackson. "I hope he didn't get his nuts twisted over it. I typed as fast as I could."

Danny has a new hair cut, truck driver short, which makes him appear taller than he is and which forms a ring of fair skin circling his head. He is the first of our unit to manage an early if thin tan, which he does by spending off-duty hours at a nearby lake. The weather has been surprisingly summery. I have observed Danny often in quarters stripped except for a posing strap. He favors navy blue, which he says highlights his skin. He has also grown a small sandy mustache, which he keeps trimmed. His one flaw, apart from a slight protrusion of his ears, is a chipped tooth which, having grown crooked, slightly overlaps the adjacent tooth and is visible when he smiles: upper right, three teeth over from the center. "It's no problem," he says. "There's no pain. And you know how these army dentists are; they'll extract rather than correct a flaw." He has strong, long-fingered hands, from "working the family ranch," he explains. There isn't much he doesn't know about horses—and cowboys, he boasts.

While he waits, I read through the major's letter, find no errors, and prepare to take it to McKinney. "Good work," I say, conscious that Jackson stands close to the desk, emphasizing his genitals.

"We should be better friends," he says. "Come to the lake on Saturday. It will still be too cold to swim. But there'll be sun."

I clear my throat. By leaning back in my chair and gazing at him, I swirl past "danger" signs. The ice is thin, the pinkish atmosphere heady and tempting. "We'll see." I meet his smile.

Later, I rationalize, saying that Jackson is simply being friendly. Seducing me will give him no advantage. He won't receive another promotion before going home; his T/5 is only three months old. We are roughly the same age, and are both Libras. I was born on October 20th, he on October 15th. There are times when I am gazing at him, when he suddenly looks up and catches me, opens his legs (if he is seated), and smiles.

That evening, anxious to see Giesela, I arrive at the club shortly after ten. She is not there.

"Tomorrow, yes," says Trudi, the woman in charge. I linger thinking that Trudi will retract what she has said, and that Giesela will materialize from the back room where employees take rest breaks.

"You hear what I say?" Trudi asks.

"Yes," I reply. I ask for a cognac and sit near the entrance. Skehan as usual is at the piano. I return his greeting. When I order another cognac, I ask Trudi if Giesela is ill.

"No, of course not," Trudi says. "She was not to be on duty. Tomorrow, I say."

I consider going to Giesela's house but think better of it. Not only is it late, but her mother won't appreciate an unannounced visit.

Trudi appears near Tom Skehan at the piano. "Special entertainment, boys," she shouts.

Skehan plays a fanfare. Curtains to the left of the bar part and out comes a female impersonator over six feet tall dressed as Carmen Miranda, complete with bare midriff, wildly colored skirt and blouse, and a hat piled with fruit. She breaks into a medley of the famous songs, including "I, I, I, I like you very much." She undulates among the tables, stroking faces, kissing, and jesting without once losing the samba beat. The timbre of the voice is perfect.

The spot moves to Skehan. His sensitive rendition of "Lili Marlene" quiets the club. Suddenly, to much applause, the impersonator returns coiffed as Dietrich. His lips are painted like Dietrich's and he wears a white fur cape, long white gloves, and a sequined gown. The voice, throaty, captures the Dietrich style. "How are you this evening, boys? Come to the back room with me. What'll you have?" Then she segues into a blend of songs. The show-stopper, of course, is "Lili Marlene." By closing my eyes, I am again in the Paris theater listening to Dietrich herself.

The next night Giesela is busier than usual since a barmaid is out sick. Nothing seems changed from what it was before we slept together. What do I expect?

Men from the headquarters baseball team, victorious over an air force group, suddenly appear, anxious to carouse. Giesela, always conscientious, doesn't take her usual break. She manages to stop at my table to say she'll be free shortly after midnight.

Later, as we step into the street (I've assumed she's going to my rooms), she draws back. "Wait, Bob, I must go to my mother's tonight."

"Is it from the bleeding?" I ask.

"No, that is not the reason." She threads her arm through mine. "Walk home with me. I am very tired."

At a small park enclosed by a wrought iron fence, we stop beneath a street lamp. Giesela's face, tilted back, has a greenish cast.

"I want to say . . . how to put it? I can't sleep with you again?" Her arms stiffen.

"I love you," I say. She won't kiss me.

"I never mean to hurt you, Bob. I never mean to."

A stab of anger. "German women are supposed to sleep with Americans." I know I'm being stupid.

"If you love me, as you say, why are you cruel? What you've just said? I thought you were different. You can't love me."

I try again to kiss her. "I'm sorry, Giesela."

"I have been thinking," she says. "Losing my blood was a negative—if that's how you say it."

I wait.

"Our men are walking to Germany from Poland and Russia. They arrive in tatters, sick as skeletons. Ten men arrive this week. My fiance Kurt is crossing Silesia. If there were no war."

"Then we'd be strangers."

When I caress her face she does not withdraw. "Giesela, go with me to America?"

She walks ahead, stops, and waits for me. "We will always be friends," she says.

"There is so little time," I remind her. "I'll be going home soon. Come with me."

"I can't, Bob. I have a family, whom I cannot leave. I love my country. And I shall marry Kurt." She clears her throat. "I feel no guilt for loving you."

We part. She enters her house. I face the door. A soft light illuminates her living room window. I turn and leave.

At headquarters I stop at my desk to inspect the latest roster for departures. Jackson's name is there. He will be leaving mid-week.

Jackson asks for a three-day pass. "I can't go to the lake tomorrow after all. I didn't expect to be going home so soon. I need to see friends in Heidelberg."

"Sure," I say, grabbing a pass form. Several had been pre-signed by the major. "I'll get someone to cover for you."

He takes the form, pausing. I place my hands on the desk, look up, and smile. I would have gone with him to the lake. "Enjoy yourself," I said.

"Look, sarge. If only we had more time . . . "

"Shall we rescind your orders?"

He laughs. "Do you care that much?"

"You won't know, will you?" I stand. "So, be off, Danny. And don't feel guilty."

"I'll be back early Tuesday. The truck for Heidelberg station leaves mid-morning Wednesday. Don't want to fuck that up."

"No, for sure."

"I'll see you Tuesday, then. It's a promise."

The headquarters building was quiet that Saturday evening. Men were either drinking at the club or viewing a Jane Russell movie in the mess hall. I took a slow bath, then tried reading some stories. I made half a dozen starts, would get to the bottom of a page, then, restless, would whip on to another, and another. My proposal: Giesela couldn't have expected the suddenness with which I flashed my metaphoric diamond. I saw a pattern to all of my various earlier proposals: proffered without warning, all were immediately rejected, the female hand raised, palm out, the slender fingers coiled in on themselves. In those earlier instances, as with Giesela, I never demurred, accepting the rejections so easily the women must have sensed that I wasn't serious in the first place. Yes, I was a sentimentalist who shivered thinking about women. What if one had accepted me?

I kicked off my bath towel and relished the cool breeze falling through the open window. This was the day that Tex and I might have gone to the lake. What was he up to with his "friends" in Heidelberg?

I sat in the chair near my bed. The room snapped. A barking dog. The whir of a passing plane. Through the window a cloud roiled etched in moonlight, caught in a huge balsam near the cemetery. My breathing was suddenly short. I slammed my fist down on the chair, rose, and hurried to the corridor and down the stairs, and into Danny's room.

Everything was in order. The cot across from his, empty now since his bunk-mate had left for home, was bare except for a neatly rolled mattress and pillow. Danny's bed was made with the sheet turned back. The sheet looked fresh. A pair of boots sat on the floor near a metal folding chair. There was a wooden armoire with a glass front, a small oval table with decorative curved legs, a pair of bath towels on a hook behind the door, a dresser covered with a comb, hairbrush, and pictures, and a padlocked GI footlocker at the foot of the bed.

I stood facing the slightly open door, imagining that Danny might return. As I stood, with my arms at my sides, listening to my breath, suspended, a redolence emerged. I quivered, catching the spoor, a sweet-and-sour scent of perspiration and human warmth, Danny's. Forming my lips, I blew streams of air, inhaling between them. Feeling giddy, I grabbed the bed pillow and buried my face in it. When I returned the pillow to the bed, I found pajama bottoms neatly folded, exuding a metallic odor of night sweat. They were black and silky. Dropping my shorts, I stepped into them, snapping them about my waist. I lay back on the bed. I was wearing Danny's skin! I edged towards the foot of the bed, tightening the cloth around my loins, pressing Danny's sweat molecules into my own pores. Then I came. After draping the pajamas over the chair to dry, I left the room.

The next evening, despite good intentions, overpowered, I found myself again in the room. Since other men were in the building, and since we had no locks or keys for our rooms, I propped a chair against the door, securing it. I rummaged through Danny's laundry bag and pulled out a posing strap. There were exudations of urine. Avidly slipping the strap over my loins, I climbed into his bed.

On leaving the room I bumped into two men on their way to the club. "Thought I heard Danny come back," I said. "You didn't see him did you?"

On Monday, Danny's immanent return kept me from his room. His pajamas would have dried (I had refolded them and returned them to their drawer); but he might be suspicious, especially if he retrieved the posing strap. I set about the day's routines which over the recent weeks were much simplified. When it became clear that our unit would soon be disbanded, formation marches to chow were cancelled, as were calisthenics. The only group obligation were morning roll calls. A permissiveness prevailed; as long as duties were performed on schedule, men could come and go as they pleased.

By mid-afternoon, I had slogged through a mass of paper work and found myself listening for sounds of Danny's return. He would probably be dropped off by one of the motor pool jeeps. His preparations for departure would take three or four hours at most: processing papers with the unit clerk, turning in equipment to supply, and packing his personal effects. Normally, since so many men were being demobilized, we threw no farewell parties—a few friends would spend the final evening drinking at the club. It was possible that I wouldn't see Danny at all, except in passing, until the morning of his departure.

He had still not returned by 4 P.M., and, restless, I left the office in charge of Greg Benson, one of the clerk typists, threw on my Ike jacket, and went to the park across the road.

Near the cemetery gates, beside the stone pillars ranged below the wrought iron inscription *Friedhof,* snow drops and violets interspersed with crocuses. Sprays of forsythia almost concealed the walls and many of the commemorative stones glistened like pearls in the dusk. Blue spruce flared near paths among the graves; the needles resembled iridescent fur. Immense castor beans thrust up poisonous spiny fruits. Blackberry brambles. A small reflecting pool, now stagnant and crammed with winter debris, shaped like a heart, glimmered, complete with cement benches to make meditation inviting.

I stood poised on the river bank, gazing down into the running water where it roiled, eroding a moss-pelfed, many-tentacled, blue-gray plane tree. For the first time since my trespass, a leathery panic appeared. Had I folded Danny's pajamas exactly as I had found them? Had I hoped that he would find me out? Taking up a stone, I flung it as far as I could, dislodging an owl that flew off with a squawk, its beak agape. *I was not a homosexual!*

At the mess hall Skehan noticed that I was preoccupied. "Snap out of it. Did you lose your fraulein?"

"That may be truer than you think," I said.

"Well, come to the club later. Wash it away with cognac. It may not last forever."

"The cognac?"

"No, your shitty mood."

Back in my room I switched the radio to U. S. Forces Radio and sat in the dark listening and waiting, for what I did not quite know. A fantasy was that Danny would walk in, close the door, and embrace me. I would not resist. Later, in the middle of a bath, I realized that I had created my own Danny. I had no real proof that he was homosexual. Was he testing me? Had I simply imagined his flirtations? Had the CO asked Danny to find me out, as he had asked me to investigate Danny? My paranoia was a mouthful of bitter grapes.

On Tuesday afternoon, Danny finally appeared, followed into my office by a tall, lithe GI with black hair fashioned in a crew cut, wearing sergeant's stripes.

"Hi," Danny greeted me, then turned to his friend. "Sarge, Devon Smith. He's with HQ in Heidelberg. We've been friends a long time. He's come to help me pack."

"So, we thought you'd decided to stay in Heidelberg," I said, with a tinge of complaint.

"I'll wait outside." Smith turned to go. "Sounds like unfinished business."

"No, No." I was being absurd. "A friend of Danny's is a friend of mine, I mean, all of us here . . . "

"There's the extra bed in my room," Danny said. "My orders are to leave tomorrow morning, right? Catch the train at noon going west."

"Well, you probably have lots to do. The clerk has papers for you to sign."

"We'll be at the club tonight. Will you be there? My treat."

"It's possible," I said. " 'Till later, then."

During the afternoon, occasional laughter moved like seductive smoke from Danny's room. The silences disturbed me. I diverted my frustration by explaining it away in religious terms. God was testing me. Sex is muscle, blood, and tissue. Self-denial is a means to personal growth. During sexual identity crises, He holds your palms to the fire, eventually withdrawing them cool and whole. Daniel among the beasts.

That evening I spent at my desk scribbling memos and writing letters home. Shortly before ten, I returned to my room, switched on Armed Forces Radio and listened quietly for nearly an hour to Glen Miller and the Andrews Sisters. I read *St. Mark.* The tiny Bible between my palms drew me into its holy pages. Calmed, I placed the book beneath my pillow and slept.

A morning of chill and drizzle. Rooks screamed chain-saw screams in a spruce across the road. The CO, dismayed, took his service revolver, went outside, and shot two of them. The remaining birds were noisier than before.

By 9:30 Danny and his friend, at the front door, waited for the jeep to Heidelberg. They had not gotten up for breakfast, or we would have said goodby at the mess hall. I motioned through the window for them to enter.

"I missed you last night," Danny said. "We didn't get back here until nearly three. I checked, but you were asleep."

"Well," I said, "you were busy."

"Did you like Devon?"

"Sure. You could be brothers."

"Other guys have said that." He lit a cigarette. "You see how it is, right? I've not fooled you."

I played dumb. "I don't know what you mean."

"OK," he said, "I won't push it."

"Is he going home today too?"

"No. Next week probably. We plan to meet in Chicago. We'll go to the university there—if we can get in on the GI Bill." He paused. "It's a lifetime thing."

"Sure."

He stood up. "Sounds like our jeep."

He stood up. He embraced me. "I do like you," he said.

Before I was aware of what he was doing, he kissed me on the mouth. "We needed more time," he said.

When he left, I stood at the window and waved goodby. I never saw him again.

I spent the next hour walking in the park. On the way back, I passed the enclosure for our trash and garbage. I slipped inside, and among Danny's discards—mostly papers, old letters, a pair of worn shoes—I found his posing strap.

In mid-March, we received word that our unit was being disbanded. We would proceed via train to Brest, France, for the return home and demobilization. On March 17th, I assembled the unit for our final march to breakfast. We had already packed our duffel bags, had policed the building, and were set to depart via truck at 9:30 at night. In Heidelberg, we boarded a long troop train filled with other GIs going home.

The journey from Heidelberg to Brest required two-and-a-half days, for we frequently sat on sidings waiting for civilian trains to pass. Whenever the train slowed, dozens of us would hang from windows yelling, urging the German engineer to speed up. At times, for miles, especially as we traversed villages and towns, motion was so slow that

Having a C-ration lunch in France on our way to Antwerp and the ship home, March, 1946.

clusters of kids assembled, running alongside, pleading for candy, gum, and cigarettes.

We by-passed Paris; I'd like to have had another glimpse of that city. At Antwerp we boarded a troop ship similar to but smaller than the one that had taken me to Southhampton months earlier. Each step up the gangplank was a step nearer home. This trip would be much shorter than the trip over; no u-boats now required that we zig-zag the Atlantic. On board were men from units throughout Europe, combatant and non-combatant. I saw a few 7th Army shoulder patches, and hoped to hear news of my old Fort Jackson unit, the 106th Division, 422nd Regiment, Company D. The lion's head on the shoulder patch was now a rainbow. The men I asked for news could tell me nothing—none had been present at Bastogne.

Other than one powerful storm on the third day out the crossing was uneventful. There were the perpetual crap games, calisthenics on deck, and much horseplay. Once the mess halls were cleared each evening, films were shown. Some men performed kitchen and mainte-

The USS *Westerly Victory* in dock at Antwerp.

nance duties. I once asembled a detail for scrubbing decks, but most of the time my tech-sergeant's stripes kept me immune from duties. Officers in charge preferred to tap regular sergeants; they were not paper pushers. It was assumed they would handle men more efficiently.

On the journey, I don't remember having any serious discussions. Nor do I recall a single GI boasting of heroism. The few wounded men aboard stayed by themselves, and those who had been prisoners of the Germans were also silent. Few men were reflective except in superficial ways—something I found true throughout my army experience. Nobody was much concerned over Hitler's fate, or what the forthcoming trials of the Nazi leaders at Nurenberg would produce. MacArthur seemed to have the Japanese under his thumb, although it was unfortunate that Hirohito remained on the throne. We saw pictures of the skeletal survivors of the nuclear holocaust and turned away, anxious to be home, to forget.

As we sailed into New York Harbor on that early misty dawn, we crammed the upper decks, screaming when we saw the Statue of Liberty and the Manhattan skyline. We expected the keys to the city. But as the ship berthed, a mere scattering of civilians, mainly longshoremen

On the crossing back to the U.S.

working on the docks, greeted us. Though combat heroes were aboard, too many had already come home to excite the public. There had been a pile-up of ships in New York and Boston harbors. We disembarked and boarded trucks bound directly for Ft. Meade, Maryland.

My honorable discharge was signed on April 6th, 1946, nearly a week after my arrival at Meade. I received travel papers for Wisconsin via train, final pay, and demobilization funds (we had changed our German marks to U. S. currency). I had about four hundred dollars in cash in my pocket. The preceding day, Tom Skehan left for St. Louis where he caught a train for California. John Ulicni and I rode to Chicago, where we parted, he to his family in the Windy City, I to Milwaukee to catch the *Chicago Northwestern* for Eagle River. Though I had sent my parents a telegram giving my estimated arrival time, I could not be sure they had received it in time since they lacked a telephone. The message would be delivered by rural mail.

6

Epilogue

EXCEPT for Fred Price, the railway platform at Eagle River was deserted. I was desperate to see my family. If Dad was not there to meet me, the walk home, though it would take less than an hour, would be anticlimactic. Amidst a noisy puff of steam the train departed for Conover and points north. I inhaled draughts of sweet highland air, then traversed the shingle-roofed station and faced the town. A Chevvie sedan was parked at the Morgan grocery with its high false front of corrugated tin. Two dwarfish Morgan brothers, each standing in separate windows, white-aproned, hands on hips, were staring at the street.

There was Dad in his bib overalls waving to me! I saw Mom, and Nell, and Jane. Jane, now nine, was wearing a dress patterned with violets and new black patent leather shoes. She clung to me. Nell, smiling, wore overalls and a flowered blouse. I remembered Mom's brown coat; but her black wide-brimmed hat was new.

"We liked all your letters," Mom said. "You gave a good idea of the boys you were with, and what the countries looked like." She felt my arm. "You've really grown."

"Yes," Dad put in. "Over six feet now."

"Six two-and-a-half," I said.

I asked about my brother.

"He's still in the army," Nell said. "Out in Oregon. I guess he'll stay now that the war's ended."

"Yes," Mom said, "he was never one for home. And the sheriff wants him for child support and bad loans. He almost never writes, and when he does it's a post card and that's it."

Everett had quit school when he was in seventh grade, after a dismal history of grades repeated and absenteeism.

101

"Remember how he'd jump off the roof of the house?" said Jane. "All you had to do was dare him, and he'd do it."

"And Marge?"

"She and Bob Kroth are living in Port Edwards where Bob grew up. He's building a house with his navy money. Margie's having a kid."

"Well," Dad said, "let's not stay here in this damp cold."

I lit a cigarette.

"I didn't know you smoked," said Mom.

"Everybody in the army smokes. The Red Cross used to give us free Camels with our doughnuts."

"All that sugar going to waste," said Nell.

The old Model A Ford, like most of Dad's cars, smelled of recycled oil. Through holes in the floorboards potholes flashed past. A piece of baling wire secured the back door, right side.

As we drove through the Sundstein District, the forests appeared far more cut-over and stunted than I remembered. The sandy soil lacked nutrients. Firs reached a meager eight feet or so. These trees browned and withered, their decomposing bark too toxic for later growth. In rare loam deposits healthier trees flourished, conveying an impression of virgin timber, before the lumber barons chopped down the great forests.

"Look there, Bob." Jane gestured. A pronged buck leaped over the road, his white-flag tail raised.

"Dad got his deer this fall," Mom said. "So you'll have a feast."

"But today it's fried chicken," Nell said. "I killed the hen."

"Yes," Mom interjected. "She's gotten good at such things. With you two boys gone, she's been the strong one."

Nell poked me in the ribs. "I'll take you on, Bob. Just say when." Her build, stocky, resembled Dad's more than Mom's. Jane was petite.

"Mom, the venison you sent me was great. I was amazed that the jar reached England in one piece, and two days before my birthday. You couldn't have timed it better. I ate it with new potatoes and green peas. I shared it with some buddies."

At Sand Corner, a mile from home, deciduous saplings had sprouted, a mix of white birch, poplar, and rough oak interspersed with pine and hemlock. Mud Creek roiled through a culvert beneath the road, broadening as it formed a new channel. Dad was proud of the spot, for he was on the WPA crew that dredged and channeled the flow. Further on, drying bogs exuded a misty dampness. Once water-logged, on their transition from marsh to woodland, they now sported blueberry shrubs. By late May or early June there would be tons of fruit, free for the picking since most of the land was owned by the county. We spent weekends picking the berries, washing them, cramming them into quart jars with a sugar syrup, and boiling them in a water bath to sterilize them for winter food.

"Today's a holiday," Dad said. "No wood chopping." He was already harvesting next winter's firewood. "I like a good start, as soon as the snow melts." He'd either drag the poles up by hand, or pile them and hire his brother's horses to portage them to the saw mill he'd made from an old Model T engine.

I asked about their lives in Sturgeon Bay where Dad had worked as a welder in the shipyards.

"We'd hoped to save money," Mom said. "The rent was high, so all we managed to do was pay off Brandner's grocery bill here."

"I did learn a trade, though," Dad said. "Before I went to the shipyard, I didn't know how to weld. I want my own shop now."

"We never get ahead," Mom complained.

Dad stopped the car below the small hill on which our house stood, near the birch-pole garage beside the driveway. The garage had lost one side and the roof was collapsed. The main house, built of logs, seemed much more decrepit than I remembered, and smaller. Though it stood a story-and-a-half high, it seemed possible to grab the metal stove pipe flanged to the tar paper roof. The logs of the oldest section, the living room, sagged, bowing in the middle, pulling the roof into a declivity which would collect snow and rain, eventually ruining the house. Dad had chinked the cracks between the logs with swamp moss, lathe, and plaster—a necessary chore preparing for the semi-Arctic winters. The paint on the front door and the window frames had peeled, and all the timbers Dad had hand-hewn for upright supports were gray. Hard yellow snow covered the front yard, although enough snow had melted near the road to attract raucous frogs. Pussy willows were out. It was still too early for mosquitoes. Beyond the house stood the cow barn, the hen house, and the toilet. The latter, like the other buildings, was of thin pine poles interspersed with birch and, like such buildings, was generic, wide enough inside for two crude seats carved from apple-box wood; a sloping roof fell off to the back to make removals of snow easy, and a nail secured a dated Sears Roebuck catalogue for wiping yourself. Nothing better symbolized our poverty than the outhouse. Yet, the military slit-trenches were worse.

Once inside the house, I climbed the uncarpeted stairs and in the attic found my old bedroom exactly as I had left it—the sagging double bed with the patchwork quilt Mom had made of heavy wool pieces arranged in a zigzag pattern, the apple box crate beside the bed holding the single-wick kerosene lamp, the pegs for clothes driven into the roof timbers, the bare roof planking with the sharpened ends of the tar paper nails securing the roof paper. Pictures from *Life* were still on the walls: Greta Garbo, Marlene Dietrich, Norma Shearer, a young rancher frozen dead, caught during a blizzard in Montana and trapped in barbed wire, and a rotogravure newspaper drawing of an imaginary wolf child captured near the Ganges. Even my old Bible had lain untouched all these months behind a faded blue cloth covering the apple box. There was also a pile of "snot rags," squares of flannel we used for hawking phlegm during winter colds.

In a large cardboard box I found my old jeans and a plaid woolen shirt. I doffed my army wear, and, though the old clothes were short in the legs, they felt good.

Downstairs Mom had a bountiful meal waiting. The chicken, breaded and fried crisp in hot bacon fat, was delicious. There were also mashed potatoes whipped airy with cream, eaten with thick brown gravy and canned string beans from the larder in the dirt cellar under the living room floor. No salad, since greens were out of season. For dessert, incredible slabs of blueberry pie (I had almost a whole pie myself) topped with blueberry ice cream churned by my sisters from ice chipped from the still-substantial ice-plates frozen near the outside well. As kids, we always strove for the dasher, since that meant you had more dollops of the ice cream than the others had.

"You take it," Nell said, handing the dasher to me.

"No, Nell. You did the work."

Later, after unpacking, I gave my unit insignias to my sisters and the ETO (European Theater of Operations) ribbon and my Good Conduct Medal to my mother. I returned Dad's knife.

"I never had to use this," I said.

He tested the blade with his finger. "It still feels sharp," he said. "I did a good job."

"I still don't know if I'd have had the guts to use it . . . "

"Well, it was there if you needed it." He suddenly bent backwards with his palm against his sacrum.

"You OK, Dad?"

"Sore back. I live with it. I'll have Ma walk on it later. That helps."

He took up the knife again. "I'll put it with my tools, in case you think you'll ever want it." Years later, I found the knife among his possessions. This was, of course, long after Mom tossed out my uniform (I still miss the Eisenhower jacket with its tech-sergeant stripes) and burned the dozens of letters I had written home. Fortunately, she saved the snapshots.

That week Dad, Nell, and I cleared brush and tilled potato patches, corn fields, and garden plots. I was very efficient in swinging an axe and using a cross cut saw. Though it was still too cold to plant seeds, we started vegetables in boxes indoors, to transplant in May. I looked after several setting hens who would leave their nesting boxes for water and food and expel noisome mounds of feces. Many hatching chicks had to be aided in breaking through their shells. I fetched them, still wet, to the house where Mom spread newspaper in the kitchen and erected a brooder made of a kerosene barn-lantern and a dome of galvanized metal that threw heat down onto the chicks.

I performed these chores readily, even avidly, but after a few days was restless. To see how little this primitive life had changed was disquieting. My family scrabbled almost as much as poor Germans made destitute by the war.

Some of my restlessness was sexual. I was a strapping youth now isolated, with no possibility of a liaison with either gender. I fantasized over Danny Jackson in Germany and Roland Stephan in England. A recurring dream transpired at the Eros Fountain in Central London where a series of females served me. Yet, when I dreamed of love as tenderness, males were the object. If, as the philosophers say, good and evil exist as polarities within each brain, why not sexual polarities?

When I first proposed to Dad that we use my army savings to buy Mom a place in town where she would have running water, electricity, and plumbing, he demurred, and, in fact, seemed hurt. I threatened his virility; he was the provider. Neither of us put this into words, and it was indeed a great step to sell the forty acres he had bought through Roosevelt's Home Owners' Loan Corporation. "I'm going to do it, Dad," I insisted.

Mom also demurred, then agreed, and one Saturday we drove to Eagle River, found a small two-story, freshly-painted, white clapboard house in the north end, on a small lot, with a garage. The house, facing an unpaved street, was being sold by the owner. The rooms were small and well-insulated. Heat was provided by an oil furnace. The electrical wiring was new and there was city water. The next step was to list the old farm with a realtor, which we did, aware that buying the new house was contingent on selling that one. A new buyer would probably want to rip the old house down and start over. That the property fronted a lake was a plus.

Within two weeks the farm sold. The small profit after the realtor's costs amounted to $1,500 which, combined with $3,000 of my savings, enabled us to buy the house in town. Within a month we moved, a fairly simple operation, since, apart from a small flock of chickens, we had no livestock. The arthritic orange dog Fido was dead, and Dad had sold the cow before moving to Door County. Dad could now start his welding business in the garage, and my sister Nell, in high school, could work at an A&W root beer stand a few blocks away.

One other gift remained to be made. My mother worried that they were too poor to buy a cemetery plot for her and Dad. I would tease her, saying that we'd carry her into the woods, dig a hole, and drop her in. She was not amused. Through the secretary of the local cemetery board, I bought a triangular plot near the park entrance for one hundred and twenty dollars. The site is large enough for two coffins and for my ashes.

At this time I also processed admission papers for the university and was accepted. I would need new clothes. Though I located two pair of trousers made of flimsy war-time gabardine, buying a suit was difficult. Priebe's Toggery, the only men's store in town, had a single possible suit in stock, a heavy, brown, worsted affair. Priebe himself (I had gone to high school with his son) promised that since he had nothing else, he would tailor the suit to fit. Civilian goods were still in short supply, he complained. It would take months before a decent stock arrived for his shelves. Priebe pinned the sleeves back, took tucks in the waist and the seat, and promised I'd be in "style." He'd have it ready next day. "Don't worry about cuffs," he said. "Cuffs went out with the war to save cloth so that you boys would have it for uniforms. They'll be wearing cuffless suits this fall, I guarantee." I paid him forty dollars and next day took the severely reshaped suit home. I wore the wretched thing a few times in Madison, then burned it in the trash. I had better luck with a brown overcoat and a stetson hat.

Late in July, Dad found an old Model A Ford for seventy-five dollars which he repaired and taught me to drive, and which eased the move to Madison where, supported by the GI Bill for three years and a month, I raced through my education. The bill took me within a month of my Ph.D. in English Literature, to my marriage in 1955, and the birth of my first child, a son, the following year.

On the last afternoon before driving south to the university, I took a long solitary walk past our old farm where the new owners were building a basement for a new house.

Tall grass flourished in the old hen yard and the pigsty. Our wood ricks were still stacked in rows for winter. Dad had also left his old saw rig behind, the machine he had engineered from the old Model T motor, a rotating belt, and a circular blade, all now rusting in the damp. The potato and corn fields lay fallow, the latter still rife with dead stalks turned a harsh yellow. I felt I could reach out and hold the farm in my hand.

I followed a trail nearly obscured by ferns and hazel brush through a deep woods tangled with undergrowth. The stream leading to Mud Minnow Lake, though low, was full enough to require care in crossing. A breeze skittered over the spot where we launched our boat. The old pier of spindly birch and pine saplings was in decay. Our boat, too leaky now for use, lay bottom up in the water. A red-winged blackbird warbled on a cattail spike. Cranberry bushes flashed pink blossoms.

I knelt on the pier, gazing into the water. Despite the heavy silt formed by mulch, I could see to the bottom, to nubby, fuzzed hemlock and oak caps lying there half buried in ooze. Three or four stunted perch suspended themselves briefly before dashing on.

Bending far over, kneeling in the frigid water covering the fragile pier, I held the flat of my hand to the green surface, bringing my palm down so slowly I felt suction between my skin and the water, the lake's integument tugging ever so gently on mine. My hand drifted slowly under, up to the elbows. I turned my arm, scooping up water and bringing it to my mouth, a communion.